Within the Circle of Light

JENNIFER WILLIAMS JUSTICE

ISBN 978-1-0980-9396-9 (paperback)
ISBN 978-1-0980-9397-6 (digital)

Christian Faith Publishing, Inc.
832 Park Avenue
Meadville, PA 16335
www.christianfaithpublishing.com

Printed in the United States of America

SECTION 1

The Poems of Life

A New Life

I was just a nobody out on my own,
for God to notice and call me home.

Though walking in darkness, sin, and strife,
Jesus still noticed and offered me life.

I stopped for a moment to consider His gift
and thought, *Where in my life would Jesus fit?*

I don't have the time, my days are quite full,
but the Spirit took notice and started to pull.

My heart swung around
one hundred and eighty degrees,

where I saw the Lord's love
and fell down on my knees.

Today's the beginning, a new life to spend
walking with Jesus forever, Amen.

Prayer for Growth

Take out the lies, Lord,
and replace them with truth.
Restore the innocence
of my youth.

Remove insecurity.
Give me trust instead.
Remind me forever
of Your words that I've read.

Keep me always
in a teachable place.
And give me the desire
to seek Your face.

Give me the ability
to do as You ask,
And the determination
to fulfill each task.

Show me the things that
are not pleasing to You.
Give me the courage
to be changed and new.

The Roadside Shanty

An old roadside shanty, with a crack in the window
stood alone without shame or pride.
Most people passed quickly not wanting to notice
or caring to see what was inside.

"It doesn't look good, it's too broken-down.
Worthless, abandoned!" they sneered.
They would not see that the shanty by a tree
was much more than it humbly appeared.

Down the road just a way where most people gathered
were houses fancy and new.
With wrought-iron gates and pretty landscapes
full of flowers of pink, yellow, and blue.

These houses look good, they are very well-built
and it's nice that they all look the same.
As they stood there admiring,
the sky had been acquiring
clouds and it started to rain.

Now out there alone, by the roadside shanty
with the window that had a crack that showed,
Were eight people who were traveling
and were caught by surprise,
by the storm as they walked down the road.

Looking for shelter, they glanced at the shanty,
next to a very old tree.
"It's dirty!" they said, "And not near good enough
for eight people as noble as we!"

"Those are for us!" as they pointed down the hill
where the new houses all stood in a row.
So they walked quickly down to the middle of town
as the wind was now starting to blow.

They were soaked to the skin
and chilled to the bone
and all were beginning to tire.
All were quite hungry and started talking of food
and expecting a warm cozy fire.

"Hurry, come with me!" cried a man out in front
and the others said they would follow.
But when they knocked on the doors,
a sad sound was heard,
they discovered the houses were hollow.

The windows were dark, they were empty inside.
There was even an unpleasant smell.
As they looked all around,
in dismay there was found,
in the back, a large bitter well.

"What shall we do, there's no place to go?
We will die if we have to stay here!"

And they huddled together in confusion and shock
and shivered, not from cold, but from fear.

In the darkness was heard a very small voice
from a child, and they all heard her plea.
"Why don't we go back to the roadside shanty,
that was standing alone by a tree?

It has to be better than standing out here.
What's one night in a rundown old shack?"
"We must," they all grumbled.
"There's no choice," they said.
So up the hill they all started back.

They stopped at the shanty. It was the same as before,
With the crack in the window and an unlocked front door.

As they pushed the door open
and they all stepped inside
they noticed the shanty was warm.
And thought it didn't seem right,
in the room there was light,
even in the midst of the storm.

An aroma was floating in the air, it smelled good,
which reminded them they hadn't been fed.
And to their surprise, in the middle of the room
was sweet water and a plate of fresh bread.

Eight folded blankets with eight pillows on top
were placed neatly along the back wall.
Eight pairs of soft slippers
and eight clean woolen robes
were there, hanging up in the hall.

All of their faces were full of great wonder

and they asked, "How can this be?
Why couldn't we see what was inside this shanty
by the roadside, next to a tree?

"Maybe it was pride that kept us from seeing inside."
Said the child with the still small voice.
"We don't deserve this, we hated this place
and to be here was not our first choice."

They all nodded their heads
as they looked around at each other
and said, "Yes, you know, she is right."
They looked at the floor and scuffled their feet,
feeling ashamed and very contrite.

When they decided to sleep, they humbly lay down
as the storm continued to rage on.
And in the morning they awoke with clear rested minds
and in their hearts they were singing a new song.

Sunshine poured in through the window with a crack
and the sky was now brilliantly blue.
Though the world hadn't changed,
as they peered through the glass,
they saw it from a new point of view.

They were not eager to leave
but had to get started.
They were excited about what they would share.
About an old roadside shanty,
that stood next to a tree

and the Love they found in it there.
And how you can't judge by the way something looks,
it could be good, even if it's a sight!

As they walked off down the road,
they all started to sing.
Much to the shanty's delight.

A Spiritual Prison

There is a terrible evil infesting the land
causing many to die by abortion on demand.

But others are wounded, perhaps bleeding for years
not knowing the real reason for all of their tears.

The destroyer seeks to take captive the women,
to lock them in chains in a spiritual prison.

Compelling the action, then accusing the same
he tortures her mind with guilt and pain.

She suffers in agony and grieves in her heart.
He takes every advantage to tear her apart.

He'll tell her to deny it, or cover it up in some way.
Or "God won't forgive you, you're gonna have to pay!"

He hates the creation God holds so dear
And it's God's love and mercy he wants her to fear.

But it was for her that God watched His only Son die,
to release her from prison, so she need not cry.

He's waiting to free her, He's holding the keys.
She need only cry out "Oh, Jesus, help me!"

He'll be there in that instant,
from God's right hand above,
to set free and start healing with forgiveness and love.

"A Spiritual Prison" scripture references

Listen to my prayer O God, do not ignore my plea; hear me and answer me. My thoughts trouble me and I am distraught at the voice of the enemy, at the stares of the wicked; for they bring down suffering upon me and revile me in their anger. My heart is in anguish within me; the terrors of death assail me. Fear and trembling have beset me; horror has overwhelmed me. I said, "Oh that I had the wings of a dove! I would fly away and be at rest—I would flee far away and stay in the desert; I would hurry to my place of shelter, far from the tempest and storm. (Psalm 55:1–8)

He was a murderer from the beginning, not holding to the truth, for there is no truth in him. When he lies, he speaks his native language, for he is a liar and the father of lies. (John 8:44)

Be self-controlled and alert. Your enemy the devil prowls around like a roaring lion looking for someone to devour. (1 Peter 5:8)

I am in the midst of lions; I lie among ravenous beasts. Man whose teeth are spears and arrows, whose tongues are sharp swords. (Psalm 5:4)

But I call to God, and the Lord saves me. Evening, morning and noon I cry out in distress, and He hears my voice. (Psalm 55:16–17)

For He will deliver the needy who cry out, the afflicted who have no one to help. He will take pity on the weak and the needy and save the needy from death. He will rescue them from oppression and violence, for precious is their blood in His sight. (Psalm 72:12–14)

For God so loved the world that He gave His one and only Son, that whoever believes in him shall not perish but have eternal life. For God did not send His Son into the world to condemn the world, but to save the world through Him. Whoever believes in Him is not condemned. (John. 3:16–18

TALK WITH GOD

In a quiet time of worship, my tears started falling.
And the Lord saw my tears, and I heard His voice calling,

"Tell me, child, why are you crying?"
"Because, Lord, it hurts to see so many dying.

"I tell them their road is going the wrong way,
but they claim they're not interested
in the things that I say.

"It doesn't seem to faze them to hear all my cries.
I'm afraid that they've listened to too many lies.

"There is joy in my heart, for by grace, I know You.
But I'm crying… I want them to feel this way too.

"Isn't there something, Lord, that I can do
that would cause Your light, in their lives, to shine through?"

"Pray for them, child. Put yourself in their place.
Cry unto me and keep seeking My face.

"Pour out your heart. Know I'm listening to you.
I tell you truly that My heart hurts too.

"It's not my desire that a single one perish
And every last one, I'm longing to cherish.

"But your prayers cause the darkness around them to flee
That they may have a chance to truly see Me."

The Heart of Bus 17

I have the heart of a servant,
I was created on purpose that way.
I willingly give every effort,
to serve children in need every day.

In the beginning, the children thought highly
of the way that I wanted to please.
But now they don't seem to take notice,
or they sneer, make judgments or tease.

It hurts when they laugh and make fun of
the way I look, now that I'm old.
The scars I do carry are many,
from wounds by hearts that are cold.

But I love the work I am doing
Even amid all the violence and pain.
And the joy I receive just from serving
is the best thing I ever could gain.

It won't be long till I'm finished
with the work I was chosen to do.
But till then I'll be doing my life's work
with a greeting of "May I help you?"

Scripture reference

> *We stand true to the Lord whether others honor us or despise us, whether they criticize us or commend us. We are honest, but they call us liars. The world ignores us but we are known to God; we live close to death, but here we are, still very much alive. We have been injured but kept from death. Our hearts ache, but at the same time we have the joy of the Lord. We are poor, but we give rich spiritual gifts to others. We own nothing, and yet we enjoy everything. (2 Corinthians 6:8–10)*

WITHIN THE CIRCLE OF LIGHT

One day I was questioning
the things of this world
and if there was meaning to life.
The next thing I knew,
I was right in the middle of
a beautiful circle of light.

At first I felt shaky and all hot inside.
I really began to feel odd.
Then my blood started racing
as I began to realize
I was in the presence of Almighty God.

I was very concerned
that this might be a dream
and that this dream was not going to last.
But then I was saddened,
I didn't feel worthy.
I was very ashamed of my past.

My tears started flowing,
I became very sorry
for even things I'd said under my breath.
for there in His presence,
that was Holy and Pure
I knew I deserved only death.

But He said, "Don't be afraid, child.
Please repent of your sins,
and a gift I'll give you for free.
You see, I love you so much
that I gave up My Son

so you could always be here with Me.
My Son died on a cross,
though He was sinless Himself,
to pay the debt you can never repay.
If you accept Him as Lord,
I'll forgive you your sins.
Come now, child, what do you say?"

I looked at His Son,
who was there by His side.
such compassion was there on His face.
And not only that,
but an intense desire that
I would always stay there in that place.

I was pierced through my heart
and said yes to the Lord,
in a small and trembling voice.
Then the circle got bigger,
a shout of joy echoed out
and I saw the angels in heaven rejoice.

I was then sealed with the Spirit
of the Living God and He's proven
to be Faithful and True.
He has cleansed me from sin.
Eternal life is His gift
and He's willing to do this for you!

Dear Lord

There is someone living down the street,
I know You know their name.
But they haven't an idea that
on the Throne of Grace You reign.

They do not know You see them
and care what happens in their life.
They do not know it hurts You
to see their suffering and strife.

They don't know how much You love them,
about Your dying on that cross.
Or that their sins were placed upon You
so that their life should not be lost.

They think they've heard about You.
And of religion they want no part.
But they haven't really heard the Truth
and it's still dark within their heart.

It hurts me too, Lord. I long to tell them
about the things You've done for me.
About how much You love them.
And Your desire to set them free.

But I don't know how to do it.
How to start or what to say.
But You know my heart is willing,
Lord, direct my steps today.

Help Me

Lonely, sad,
angry, just mad.
I have all of these feelings inside.

Fearful, confused.
Tired of feeling used.
I wish I could just go and hide.

My heart feels like breaking.
There's a longing, and aching
deep down in my soul.

I'm needing, I'm wanting.
But what? It's just haunting.
I feel like I'm not really whole.

I feel like I'm dying.
I wish I were crying,
but the tears just don't seem to be there.

Feeling the worse for wear.
Full of hopeless despair.
I don't know if I really do care.

Lord, help me today
I can't find my way.
It seems scary and dark, way down here.

I'll stand on Your Word.
And quote verses I've heard
where You promise to always be near.

It seems with You I've lost touch.
And I miss You so much.
Hear my voice when I cry unto You.

Give me courage to stand.
Lord, take hold of my hand.
Help me, Lord… I'm feeling so blue.

IF IT WERE JUST ME

If it were just me
that responded to Your voice,
Would You have come anyway
to give me that choice?

If it were just me
that would answer Your call,
Would You still have left heaven?
Would You have left it all?

If just me were to praise You
with my every breath,
Would You still have chosen
that road to death?

Would You have died on that cross,
on that hill, Calvary?
If from the whole world,
You redeemed only me?

You say that You would have,
Your word says it's true.
That God loves us so much
that He gave us You.

And that whoever believes in You,
He would give
A free gift, the right to eternally live.

Oh, thank you, Jesus, for sure now I know,
If it were just me, You would not have said no!

Learning to Fight

As a baby is my spirit
I took whatever life would bring.
I believed what people told me
and never questioned anything.

As a child in my spirit,
I saw that not all things were right.
I didn't know that this was war
and that I had to learn to fight.

While confused by words and actions,
a Warrior appeared within the feud.
He handed me a tiny sword
and said, "Do what I do!"

Standing right in front of me
I was shielded from where He stood.
And we practiced using weapons,
though I wasn't very good.

As a teen in my spirit, I used my sword
for big battles, or so I thought.
But again the Warrior appeared to me,
and with Him, a gift He brought.

He replaced my sword with a bigger one.
The sword of the Spirit, of which I've read.
He prepared me for battle with armor
The helmet of salvation He placed on my head.

He stood directly behind me,
and told me, "Do not be afraid.

The victory is Mine, the battle is won
For your life, the ransom's been paid.

But the enemy does not back down easily.
His pride blinds him to all of these facts.
So I've given you the weapons of warfare.
Be prepared, for you will be attacked.

Just remember that I'm with you always.
To teach you things you need at that time.
And know that I love you completely.
I rejoice in knowing you're mine!"

"Learning to Fight" scripture references

> *When I was a child, I talked like a child, I thought like a child, I reasoned like a child. When I became a man, I put childish ways behind me. (1 Corinthians 13:11)*

> *Consider it pure joy, my brothers, whenever you face trials of many kinds, because you know that the testing of your faith develops perseverance. Perseverance must finish its work so that you may be mature and complete, not lacking anything. (James 1:2–5)*

> *We wait in hope for the Lord; He is our help and our shield. (Psalm 33:20)*

> *Stand firm then, with the belt of truth buckled around your waist, with the breastplate of righteousness in place, and with your feet fitted with the readiness that comes from the gospel of peace. In addition to all this, take up the shield of faith, with which you can extinguish all the flaming arrows of the evil one. Take the helmet of salvation and*

the sword of the Spirit, which is the word of God. (Ephesians 6:14–17)

Are not two sparrows sold for a penny? Yet not one of them will fall to the ground apart from the will of your Father. And even the very hairs of your head are all numbered. So don't be afraid; you are worth more than many sparrows. (Matthew 10:29–31)

But thanks be to God! He gives us the victory through our Lord Jesus Christ. (1 Corinthians 15:57)

For there is one God and one mediator between God and men, the man Christ Jesus, who gave himself as a ransom for all men. (1 Timothy 2:5–6)

Put on the full armor of God so that you can take your stand against the devil's schemes. For our struggle is not against flesh and blood, but against the rulers, against the authorities, against the powers of this dark world and against the spiritual forces of evil in the heavenly realms. Therefore put on the full armor of God, so that when the day of evil comes, you may be able to stand your ground, and after you have done everything, to stand. (Ephesians 6:11–13)

And surely I am with you always, to the very end of the age. (Matthew 28:20)

The Lord your God is with you, He is mighty to save. He will take great delight in you, He will quiet you with His love, He will rejoice over you with singing. (Zephaniah 3:17)

Longing to Know

Walking in meadows, up mountains or hills,
I'm walking wherever the Spirit of God wills.

Trudging through deserts or strolling by creeks,
I'll listen whenever the Spirit of God speaks.

I'll go into swampland and push through the reeds.
I'm willing to go where the Spirit of God leads.

Though it's frightening to see quicksand as I walk,
I'm trusting the Spirit to show me the "Rock."

When it's dark in the valleys, on the pathways at night,
I know the Spirit of God will be revealing "The Light."

While gaining a respite along sandy beaches,
I'm longing to know what the Spirit of God teaches.

I'm open, I'm willing to put Jesus first.
I feel the spirit of God quenching my thirst.

"Longing to Know" scripture reference

> *Show me Your ways, O Lord.*
> *Teach me Your paths. Lead me*
> *in Your truth and teach me. For*
> *You are the God of my salvation.*
> *On You I wait all the day! (Psalm 25:4–5)*

Patterns

The patterns in our mind reveal
the things our hearts and spirits feel.

Things harbored down inside too long
cause patterns to become all wrong.

Formed by lies they sometimes gain
a way to cause us guilt and pain.

They build up walls, the structures stand,
but all of them are on the sand.

Built upon this shaky ground,
the patterns cause our hearts to pound.

Fears engulf our reasoning mind,
tormenting us with thoughts that bind.

Fears of God. Fears of men.
Fears of everything, but then;

Deep inside, a remembered thought.
A pattern built upon a rock.

The walls come down, the structures too.
The patterns now are made brand-new!

"Patterns" scripture references

*There is a way that seems right to a man, but in the
end it leads to death. (Proverbs 14:12)*

But the things that come out of the mouth came from the heart, and these make a man unclean. For out of the heart come evil thoughts, murder, adultery, sexual immorality, theft, false testimony, and slander. (Matthew 15:18)

For if you forgive men when they sin against you, your heavenly Father will also forgive you. But if you do not forgive men their sins, your Father will not forgive your sins. (Matthew 6:14)

Watch out for false prophets. They come to you in sheep's clothing, but inwardly they are ferocious wolves. (Matthew 7:15)

Therefore everyone who hears these words of mine and puts them into practice is like a wise man who built his house on the rock. The rain came down, the streams rose, and the winds blew and beat against that house; yet it did not fall, because it had its foundation on the rock.

But everyone who hears these words of mine and does not put them into practice is like a foolish man who built his house on sand. The rain came down, the streams rose, and the winds blew and beat against that house, and it fell with a great crash. (Matthew 7:24–27)

Do not conform any longer to the patterns of this world, but be transformed by the renewing of your mind. (Romans 12:2)

QUESTIONS AND ANSWERS

Lord, how do You keep
from flooding the earth with Your tears,
caused by the wickedness
of man through all of his years?

For all that he touches
is then tainted with evil and sin,
from the depths of his heart
is an enemy living within.

How can You love one
as ugly and filthy as he?
So much that You'd send
Your Son Jesus to die on a tree?

"My thoughts are not your thoughts, My ways are not your
ways," You say.
"And the things of this world
will soon be passing away.

But the joy I receive from a child,
one such as you,
who was lost as the others,
but found and then made brand-new,

Is a treasure I cherish,
and the world will not perish,
until every child that I've called
has come home."

"Questions and Answers" scripture references

As it is written: "There is no one righteous, not even one; there is no one who understands, no one who seeks God. All have turned away, they have together become worthless, there is no one who does good, not even one. Their throats are open graves; their tongues practice deceit. The poison of vipers is on their lips. Their mouths are full of cursing and bitterness. Their feet are swift to shed blood; ruin and misery mark their ways, and the way of peace they do not know. There is no fear of God before their eyes." (Romans 3:10–18)

Let the wicked forsake his way and the evil man his thoughts. Let him turn to the Lord, and he will have mercy on him, and to our God, for he will freely pardon. "For my thoughts are not your thoughts, neither are your ways My ways," declares the Lord. "As the heavens are higher than the earth, so are My ways higher than your ways and My thoughts than your thoughts. As the rain and the snow come down from heaven, and do not return to it without watering the earth and making it bud and flourish, so that it yields seed for the sower and bread for the eater, so is My word that goes out from My mouth: It will not return to Me empty, but will accomplish what I desire and achieve the purpose for which I sent it." (Isaiah 55:7–11)

The Lord delights in those who fear Him, who put their hope in His unfailing love. (Psalm 146:11)

For the Lord takes delight in His people, He crowns the humble with salvation. (Psalm 149:4)

Reality Is...

People are dying all over the earth,
but it's not just a physical death.

Even though they don't feel it, their spirits
are strangling, each time they take a new breath.

Their spirits are broken, bleeding and bound up
in chains. They are naked, wretched and poor.

But they say they are fine. Or just leave me alone,
I don't need anything more.
Except maybe more money, or a shiny new car,
A new house or a fancy new job.

They have no idea that for the life of their souls,
Satan will destroy, kill or rob.

But those of us who are in the Kingdom of God
can see the terrible danger they're in.

And if we don't take some action to point the way
to our Lord, in their case, the enemy will win!

"Reality Is..." scripture references

> *Because you say, "I am rich, and have become*
> *wealthy, and have need of nothing," and you do*
> *not know that you are wretched and miserable and*
> *poor and blind and naked, I advise you to buy from*
> *Me gold refined by fire, that you may become rich,*
> *and white garments, that you may clothe yourself*
> *and that the shame of your nakedness may not be*

revealed; and eye salve to anoint your eyes, that you may see. Those whom I love, I reprove and discipline; be zealous therefore, and repent. Behold, I stand at the door and knock; if anyone hears My voice and opens the door, I will come in to him, and dine with him, and he with Me. (Revelation 3:17–20)

Jesus therefore said to them again, "Truly, truly, I say to you, I am the door of the sheep. All who came before Me are thieves and robbers; but the sheep did not hear them. I am the door; if anyone enters through Me, he shall be saved, and shall go in and out, and find pasture. The thief comes only to steal and kill, and destroy; I came that they might have life and have it abundantly." (John 10:7–10)

Someone We Need

Inside everyone is a real basic need.
That's for someone to follow
or someone to lead.

We need someone to follow
when the going gets tough.
Who can point out the way
when the roadway is rough.

We need someone to lead,
who knows the way that is best.
Who can tell when we're tired
and in need of a rest.

We need someone to follow
who's willing to protect.
Whose life, in our own lives
we want to reflect.

We need someone to lead
who's been where we want to go.
Though we haven't been there,
it's a place that they know.

We need someone to follow
who hears our voice when we cry.
And is willing to listen
when we're asking them why.

We need someone to lead.
We need a perfect one.
We need to follow Christ Jesus,
God's perfect Son.

THE CHOICE OF THE SHEEP

There once was a dragon with red fiery eyes,
Who loved to fly through the nighttime skies.
Her skin was a deep shade of emerald green.
Her claws were quite sharp and she kept them real clean.

She lived in a cave that was high on a hill.
And her dinner each week was a sheep that she'd kill.
The sheep lived below where there weren't many trees
And the dragon would go there whenever she'd please.

Sometimes she would scare them, just to have fun,
swooping and screaming to just see them run.
The sheep lived in terror, they didn't sleep much,
for worrying about who'd be the dragon's next lunch.

One day while the ground was still covered with frost,
a shepherd came looking for sheep that were lost.
When he rounded a bend, he watched in dismay,
as the dragon swooped down on her intended prey.

The appearance of the shepherd made
the green dragon miss.
Which made her so angry, she started to hiss.
He said, "Why are you angry, and in such a bad mood?"
She hissed, "Shepherds like you keep taking my food!

"The sheep came here by choice,
I didn't steal them, you see.
And now here you are, to take them from me."
The shepherd stood thinking
under the dragon's cold stare.
Then said, "I want to do what we both think is fair.

"Since they came here by choice,
they could choose to leave.
So let's ask them to choose now between you and me."
The dragon replied, "I wasn't hatched yesterday!
You know they'll pick you. They won't want to stay.

"I stomp them and chomp them, and tear them to bits.
And the rest of the time they're scared out of their wits."
Said the shepherd, "Not many will come when I call,
because being with me they must surrender their all.

"Some want to be free to do the things that they choose.
But the risk that they take is their life that they lose.
Truly I tell you, you'll be left here with some.
Though I'd rather you'd not receive even one."

The dragon just glared, arrogantly cocking her head.
Then whipping her tail, she vehemently said,
"I'm not in the habit of trusting shepherds, you see.
But I'll take a chance, so yes, I agree.

"You go and ask them if they'll go home with you.
And I'll wait on my hill to see if your words are true."
The shepherd walked down
to meet the sheep where they were.
And they all asked him cautiously, "Who are you, sir?"

"I am a shepherd, and I'm seeking lost sheep.
Ones that will love me, ones I can keep.
Sheep that are tired and in need of a rest.
Sheep that will want me to give them my best.
Sheep that are willing to go where I lead.
Ones that will trust me to provide what they need.
Sheep that surrender themselves unto me.
Whom of you now will come follow me?"
A lot of the sheep had a skeptical face.

And a few, feeling uncomfortable, started to pace.
They said, "Some of us like things the way that they are
and we don't wish to travel around, near or far.

"We don't need a shepherd that won't give us our way.
And we don't want to do things the way that you say.
And some of us think a better shepherd will come.
For your way appears to be incredibly dumb.

"We don't think your way is really the best.
But we speak for ourselves and not for the rest."
A few sheep were left who hadn't spoken a word.
But they thought about all of the things that they heard.

They remembered the dragon,
and the way that she was
when she swooped down screaming,
with her razor-sharp claws.

They said, "We'll come with you,
right now, yes this night.
We believe you will save us from our deadly plight."

The shepherd repeated the things he had said.
But the others just walked away, shaking their heads.
The shepherd then kneeled, bowed his head, and he prayed.
Giving thanks to the Lord for the ones
that had stayed.

The dragon just watched, rolling her eyes in her head.
Hating the shepherd and wishing him dead.
She was dreadfully hungry and wanting to feed.
Then she saw a few sheep following that good
shepherd's lead.

She thought, "Where are the others?
He must have hid them somewhere.
I think I'll fly down there
and give them all a good scare!"

The shepherd, now, could no longer be found.
But the dragon dived down
toward the sheep on the ground.

The sheep started screaming and were in a panicky state.
And all were now crying for the shepherd to wait.
But the shepherd had gone. Their opportunity had passed.
So the dragon had two sheep for dinner, at last!

THE COLOR OF SPIRITUAL DAYS

Days that are clear are colored in white.
And everything present is washed in bright light.
Prayer is happy, a joyful song.
It seems like nothing could ever go wrong.
Perfume and music float through the air,
and for all the world we have not a care.

Days that are cloudy are colored in gray.
And things will start happening as soon as we pray.
Light may cut through the thickened sky.
Or maybe the clouds will start to cry.
But persistence in prayer gives opportunities
for rainbows that our spirit sees.

Days that are black are the ones that seem dry.
When despair fills our hearts and we ask The Lord why.
We can't see the light at the end of the tunnel
Our lives seem to swirl about inside a funnel.
But prayer on the black days reach the heart of God, too.
And with faith all that darkness will begin to turn blue.

Blue days are peaceful, quiet and subdued.
While the lessons from black days are being reviewed.
Calm washes over from the storms of gray days.
And the Lord gives us rest as we give Him praise.
Unburdened by problems or worries or fear,
the blue days begin to turn perfectly clear.

THE GOSPEL

Jesus was born in the town of Bethlehem
when the first census was taken
to count all men.
But He was alive even before His birth.
You see, He created the heavens
and all of the earth.

He is responsible for all
the good things you see.
He is responsible for creating you and me.
He was thrilled in His heart
as He was thinking of
the children He was making
that could give Him love.

He gave them free wills
so they could choose their own way.
And He hoped they would choose Him,
choose love and would stay.
But another creation,
who had fallen from grace,
looked on in disgust, with hate on his face.

Biding his time, he patiently waited
for a chance to ruin what Jesus created.
From clay Christ formed Adam
and Eve from his rib,
And He created a garden,
a place they could live.

In the center was a tree
that stretched up toward the sky.

And the Lord warned
"Don't eat of it or else you will die!"
"Did God really say you would die if you eat?
No, He was lying, it is really a treat!

"He knows you'll be able
to tell right from wrong.
You will be like Him.
You will be just like God!"

The fallen creation, the devil's his name,
was having great fun at this tempting game.
He convinced the woman
that it would be all right,
so she picked some fruit and took a big bite.

She gave some to the man
and he too ate some.
Then the Father, in sorrow, said,
"What have you done?"

"Because of this sin, you cannot remain
in this beautiful garden,
and there's going to be pain.
Hardship and trials and death you will see
because you ate from that fruit,
you disobeyed Me."

Fellowship was lost between God and man
and something was needed
to bridge this great span.
Only something good and totally pure
could be accepted by God to be a cure.

God the Father and Jesus discussed a plan
that could fulfill the requirement

to save all man.
Jesus cried because
of the price He would pay.
But He knew that to save us,
it was the only way.

So for a while He left Heaven,
with its splendor and might
and through a virgin became a baby,
one dark starry night.

He grew into manhood
as a carpenter's son
in a small town where
everyone knew everyone.

At age thirty His work
as a carpenter was done,
and He started to work
on the reason He'd come.
Baptized in the Jordan,
He heard the Father's praise.
But was sent to the desert
to be tempted forty days.

Tempted in all ways, as we are, as men,
He was tempted by Satan but He did not sin.
He then started a three-year intense ministry
that would ultimately lead Him to Calvary.

As He traveled He chose
twelve unlikely men.
And among them a tax man
and four fishermen
to be constant companions,

disciples He said,
and they watched Him heal sickness
and raise folks from the dead.

He healed the diseases
and gave sight to the blind.
Even cast out some demons
that were harming mankind.
He taught them of God
and about His great love.
And that soon He'd be returning
to heaven above.

The religious leaders
liked to make all the rules
and they thought Jesus
was making them out to be fools.
But Jesus, through all of their
mocking and taunts,
was trying to show them
what God really wants.

When the time finally came,
when the hour drew near,
Jesus prayed in the garden
with many great tears.
"If there is any other way
that saving man can be done…
but not my will, Father,
only Yours be done."

The leaders from town
came to the garden with might
but Jesus surrendered without any fight.
He willingly followed,
He chose nothing to say.

So they sentenced Him to die
on a cross the next day.

They beat Him, spit on Him, and placed thorns
on His head.
Then nailed Him to a cross,
where He hung until dead.
Though innocent of sin, He died on the tree
to pay the price for our sins,
to save you and me.

His friends took Him down,
put Him inside a tomb.
And they left full of grief,
overwhelmed by gloom.
The devil, you remember, the fallen one?
Was delighted, he killed Jesus,
he thought he had won.

He forgot that Jesus had never once sinned.
That's why death couldn't keep Him
in the tomb He was in.
So on the third day after His horrible death,
the stone rolled from the entrance
and He took a deep breath.

Life returned to His body
and He walked out of that grave
with great joy in His heart
for the men He could save.
He appeared to His men,
after being raised from the dead
and told them to tell everyone
the things He had said.

But to wait a few days,
because a helper He'd send
to dwell inside every believer
until the time of the end.
The Holy Spirit descended
as Jesus returned to His throne,
to seal each believer
as the Lord's very own.

He'll be coming again soon,
in fact it could be today
to destroy every evil
and to stop men's wicked ways.
He'll have the Lamb's Book of Life,
with every name written in
of every sinner who asked Jesus
to forgive them of sin.

Is your name in that book?
Or are you so filled with hate
that you'll see the lake of fire
and not pearly gates?
Even if you are good,
and you'd never hurt a fly

You can't get to heaven
without Jesus inside.

Jesus became the bridge
over that gigantic span
so God could have a relationship
with His much loved "Man."
It's His blood that washes away a man's sins.
This is true, so believe it. Invite Jesus in!

THE RIGHT CHOICE

Some people worship forests of beautiful trees
with various bark and colorful leaves.
They say each has a spirit living within
and to cut them down would be a great sin.
To hug one, some travel with tents and backpacks,
but I've never once seen a tree hug one back.

Some people say eagles are gods that can fly.
With glorious wings they glide through the sky.
They pray to it, asking for courage and power
and gather its feathers for a ceremonial hour.
Most live in high places, large trees, cliffs and such.
But what good is a god you can't reach out and touch?

Some people worship beings
they've carved from stone
and place them in gardens or inside their home.
They ask them for guidance or to heal a disease
chanting and praying to soothe and appease.
But that stone cannot hear them,
nor is it capable of
producing an answer of giving them love.

Still there are others who say we're all gods,
that we are all connected and should not be at odds.
And the answers we seek are inside of our minds.
And that we have the power
to change things of all kinds.
But how lonely they must feel
when they need comfort and care,
and they can't find those answers,
'cause inside they're not there.

But yet there are those who pray in their hearts
to a God who does hear them
and they're never apart.
They can reach out and touch Him
any evening or day.
And He gives them the answers
to the prayers that they pray.
He hugs them and loves them,
and they hear His voice.
For He cares for them deeply,
they have made the right choice.

Inside every man is the knowledge of God
but when that knowledge is rejected,
they worship a fraud.
Christ Jesus is God's only begotten Son
who gave up His life to save everyone.
He died, was buried and rose the third day.
And only those who believe this
will forever be saved!

"The Right Choice" scripture reference

> *As the scripture says it, "The man who finds life will find it through trusting God." But God shows his anger from heaven against all sinful, evil men who push away the truth from them.*
>
> *For the truth about God is known to them instinctively; God has put this knowledge in their hearts. Since earliest times men have seen the earth and sky and all God made, and have known of His existence and great eternal power. So they will have no excuse when they stand before God at Judgment day. Yes, they knew about Him all right, but they wouldn't admit it or worship Him or even thank Him for all His daily care. And after awhile they began to think up silly ideas of what God was like and what He wanted them to do. The result was that their foolish minds became dark and confused, claiming themselves to be wise without God, they became utter fools instead. And then, instead of worshiping the glorious, ever-living God, they took wood and stone and made idols for themselves, carving them to look like mere birds and animals and snakes and puny men.*
>
> *So God let them go ahead into every sort of sex sin, and so whatever they wanted to—yes, vile and sinful things with each other's bodies. Instead of believing what they knew was the truth about God, they deliberately chose to believe lies. So they prayed to the things God made, but wouldn't obey the blessed God who made these things. (Romans 1:17–25)*

Things That Matter

Within the Circle of Light, I felt
total acceptance, comfort, and love.

But it wasn't from any works I'd done.
Just simply for who I was.

It didn't matter my age or color of
my skin, or where I happened to live.

It didn't matter if I was poor,
or if I was able to work,
or if I had money to give.

The only things that mattered
were the things in my heart,
and if I'd repented of sin.

And if I knew Jesus as Savior and Lord.
And in my life, that I'd invited Him in.

TODAY

Today is a day unlike any other day,
for God created it new just now.
And with joy in my heart, I kneel by my bed.
With thanksgiving, my head does bow.

It's not like yesterday,
and it won't be like tomorrow.
For as yet there's no troubles
or trials or sorrows.

I'm not sure if it's raining
or if it will be bright
with the sun.
for my window's still dark.
The morning's just begun.

But I'm excited about today,
for I know God
is in command.
And I'll not fear anything,
He's got hold of my hand.

What Is Christmas?

Is it writing a gift list with vigor and zeal
to someone who is jolly but not really real?

Is it once-a-year greetings to people by mail,
or running around for that bargain or sale?

Is it parties with eggnog and holiday cheer,
or smiling at strangers without any fear?

Is it evergreen trees all dressed up with lights,
or walking and singing on cold winter nights?

Is it gifts that are given wrapped in ribbons and bows,
while yule logs burn bringing warmth to our toes.

All of these things are now parts of the season,
but none of these things explain the real reason.

God gave us a gift twenty centuries ago,
and this one came wrapped up in swaddling clothes.

He gave us the best gift a Father could give,
The one that would let Him say "Yes, I forgive!"

The birth of Christ Jesus is why we remember
the twenty-fifth day in the month of December.

"What is Christmas?" scripture reference

> *Therefore the Lord himself will give you a sign: "the virgin will be with child and will give birth to a son, and will call him Immanuel." (Isaiah 7:14)*

> *For to us a child is born, to us a son is given, and the government will be on his shoulders. And he will be called Wonderful, Counselor, Mighty God, Everlasting Father, Prince of Peace. (Isaiah 9:6)*

> *This is how the birth of Jesus came about: His mother Mary, was pledged to be married to Joseph, but before they came together, she was found to be with child through the Holy Spirit. Because Joseph her husband was a righteous man and did not want to expose her to public disgrace, he had in mind to divorce her quietly.*

> *But after he had considered this, an angel of the Lord appeared to him in a dream and said, "Joseph, son of David, do not be afraid to take Mary home as your wife, because what is conceived in her is from the Holy Spirit. She will give birth to a son and you are to give him the name Jesus, because he will save his people from their sins."*

> *All this took place to fulfill what the Lord had said through the prophet: "The virgin will be with child and will give birth to a son, and they will call him Immanuel which means, 'God with us.'"*

> *When Joseph woke up, he did what the angel of the Lord had commanded him and took Mary home as his wife. But he had no union with her until she gave birth to a son, and he gave him the name Jesus. (Matthew 1:18–24)*

> *In those days Caesar Augustus issued a decree that a census should be taken of the entire Roman world. (This was the first census that took place while*

Quirinius was governor of Syria. And everyone went to his own town to register. So Joseph also went up from the town of Nazareth in Galilee to Judea, to Bethlehem, the town of David, because he belonged to the house and line of David. He went there to register with Mary, who was pledged to be married to him and was expecting a child. While they were there, the time came for the baby to be born, and she gave birth to her firstborn, a son. She wrapped him in cloths and placed him in a manger, because there was no room for them in the inn. And there were shepherds living out in the fields nearby, keeping watch over their flocks at night. An angel of the Lord appeared to them, and the glory of the Lord shone around them, and they were terrified. But the angel said to them, "Do not be afraid. I bring you good news of great joy that will be for all the people. Today in the town of David a Savior has been born to you. He is Christ the Lord. This will be a sign to you: You will find the baby wrapped in cloths and lying in a manger." Suddenly a great company of the heavenly host appeared with the angel, praising God and saying "Glory to God in the highest, and on earth peace to men on whom his favor rests." (Luke 2:1–14)

For God so loved the world that he gave his one and only son, that whoever believes in him shall not perish but have eternal life. (John 3:16)

Who Am I?

Who am I? What am I? Why am I here?
Why am I wandering around on this sphere?

Is there purpose to life? Do I mean anything?
Does somebody love me? Is there worth to my being?

Oh, the loneliness, the desperate sorrow.
Will anyone know that I'm here, tomorrow?

The darkness and heartache, the painful despair.
Tell me now, really, does anyone care?

The terrors in shadows, confusion and fear.
When I cry out, does anyone hear?

My strength's fading quickly, my spirit is weak.
If these questions have answers, please, somebody speak!

These questions have answers. I know they are true.
And I've anchored my life in what I'm sharing with you.

We've been created by God for His perfect plan.
For His good pleasure, He created man.

He knows of our pain, He's concerned about strife.
He wants us to have an abundant life.

Though we've fallen because of the evil one,
God loves us so much that He gave us His son.

He offers us Jesus, as a ransom for sin.
For eternal life, He's the only way in.

He calls to us gently, He holds out His arms.
He wants to protect us from all kinds of harm.

To God we have value, immeasurable worth.
When we say yes to Jesus, we experience a rebirth.

We become His children, because He hears us cry,
And we are born to the family of God Most High.

"Who Am I?" scripture references

> *When God created man, He created them male and female and blessed them. And when they were created, he called them "man." (Genesis 5:1)*

> *In Him we were also chosen, having been predestined according to the plan of Him who works out everything in conformity with the purpose of His will. (Ephesians 1:11)*

> *Cast all your anxiety on Him because he cares for you. (1 Peter 5:7)*

> *The thief comes only to steal and kill and destroy; I came that they might have life, and might have it abundantly. (John 10:10)*

For all have sinned and fall short of the glory of God. (Romans 3:23)

For God so loved the world that He gave his one and only son, that whoever believes in him shall not perish but have eternal life. (John 3:16)

For there is one God and one mediator between God and men, the man Christ Jesus, who gave himself as a ransom for all men. (1 Timothy 2:5–6)

I am the way and the truth and the life. No one comes to the Father except through me. (John 14:6)

I revealed myself to those who did not ask for me; I was found by those who did not seek me. To a nation that did not call on my name. I said "Here I am, Here I am…" All day long I have held out my hands to an obstinate people, who walk in the ways not good, pursuing their own imaginations. (Isaiah 65:1–2)

"Because he loves me," says the Lord, "I will rescue him; will protect him, for he acknowledges my name. He will call upon me, and I will answer him; I will be with him in trouble, I will deliver him and honor him. With long life will I satisfy him and show him my salvation." (Psalm 91:14–16)

Consider the ravens: They do not sow or reap, they have no storeroom or barn: yet God feeds them. And how much more valuable you are than birds! (Luke 12:24)

The kingdom of heaven is like treasure hidden in a field. When a man found it, he hid it again, and then in his joy went and sold all he had and bought that field. Again, the kingdom of heaven is like a merchant looking for fine pearls. When he found one of great value, he went away and sold everything he had and bought it. (Matthew 13:44–45)

I tell you the truth, no one can enter the kingdom of God unless he is born of water and the Spirit. Flesh gives birth to flesh, but the Spirit gives birth to spirit. (John 3:5–7)

Everyone who believes that Jesus is the Christ is born of God. (1 John 5:1)

Yet to all who received him, to those who believed in his name, he gave the right to become children of God—children born not of natural descent, nor of human decision or a husband's will, but born of God. (John 1:12–13)

WILLINGLY

I lay my life on your altar, Lord
I willingly give it to You.

I believe the words that You've given me.
I know You are faithful and true.

My life, by itself, leads me nowhere
but to death and lonely despair.

But with You I have joy overflowing
and I'm comforted knowing You're there!

"Willingly" scripture references

Submit yourselves, then, to God. Resist the devil, and he will flee from you. Come near to God and he will come near to you. (James 4:7)

If anyone would come after me, he must deny himself and take up his cross and follow me. For whoever wants to save his life will lose it, but whoever loses his life for me and for the gospel will save it. (Mark 8:34–35)

Know therefore that the Lord your God is God; He is the faithful God, keeping his covenant of love to a thousand generations of those who love him and keep his commands. (Deuteronomy 6:9)

There is a way that seems right to a man, but in the end it leads to death. (Proverbs 14:12)

For death is the destiny of every man; the living should take this to heart. (Ecclesiastes 6:2)

You have make known to me the path of life; you will fill me with joy in your presence, with eternal pleasures at your right hand. (Psalm 16:11)

For You, O Lord, have helped me and comforted me. (Psalm 86:17)

Praise be to the God and Father of our Lord Jesus Christ, the Father of compassion and the God of all comfort, who comforts us in all our troubles, so that we can comfort those in any trouble with the comfort we ourselves receive from God. (2 Corinthians 1:3–4)

And surely I am with you always, to the very end of the age. (Matthew 28:20)

THE LIGHTHOUSE

If the lighthouse didn't shine it's light,
Where would the travelers be?
When on their ship they sailed too close to the rocks
Hidden under the sea

And where would the little wooden ship be
When tossed and battered by the storm
If it couldn't see the light from the lighthouse tower
And it failed to blow its horn?

Though they might make it past
The shoal of rocks
To the Harbor
Where they would find rest,

Seeing the tower of light
Or hearing its horn
Was the way that
Would have served them best.

What Was It?

What was it about that simple man
That people loved so much?

The words he spoke with authority,
Or the healing in his touch?

What was it about that common man
That drew people to his side?

The compassion he had on the people,
Or his uncommon joy deep inside?

What was it about that innocent man
That some people turned to despise?

The knowledge he had of their lifestyle,
Or the forgiveness in his eyes?

What was it about that humble man
that caused some men to stumble and fall?

But others to give up their livelihood,
To drop everything to answer his call?

What was it about that gentle man
Who was acquainted with sorrow and grief?

That would cause him to willingly suffer and die
Once for all in the place of a thief?

What was it about the sinless man
That for sin he would die in our place?

Not only that but to forgive us those sins
And pour out on us his love and grace?

What was it about that Godly man
That would cause him to rise from the dead?

So that those who believe would not die in their sins,
But with Him live forever instead?

"What Was It?" scripture reference

> *They were all amazed, so that they debated among themselves, saying, "What is this? A new teaching with authority! He commands even the unclean spirits, and they obey Him." (Mark 1:27)*

Speaking of the Lord:

> *Who redeems your life from the pit, Who crowns you with lovingkindness and compassion. (Psalm 130:4)*

> *The fear of the Lord is the beginning of knowledge; Fools despise wisdom and instruction. (Proverbs 1:7)*

> *Whoever is wise, let him understand these things; Whoever is discerning, let him know them. For the ways of the LORD are right, And the righteous will walk in them, But transgressors will stumble in them. (Hosea 14:9)*

> *As He passed by, He saw Levi the son of Alphaeus sitting in the tax booth, and He said to him, "Follow Me!" And he got up and followed Him. (Mark 2:14)*

He was despised and rejected by men; a man of sorrows, and acquainted with grief, and as one from whom men hide their faces he was despised, and we esteemed him not. (Isaiah 53:3)

Pilate said to Him "What is truth?" And when he had said this he went out again to the Jews and said to them, "I find no guilt in Him. But you have a custom that I release someone for you at the Passover; do you wish then that I release for you the King of the Jews?" so they cried out again, saying "not this Man, but Barabbas." Now Barabbas was a robber. (John 18:38–40)

And he died for all, that those who live should no longer live for themselves but for him who died for them and was raised again. (2 Corinthians 5:15)

So that being justified by His grace we would be made heirs according to the hope of eternal life. (Titus 3:7)

And to wait for His Son from heaven, whom He raised from the dead, that is Jesus, who rescues us from the wrath to come. (1 Thessalonians 1:10)

For God so loved the world, that He gave His only begotten Son, that whoever believes in Him shall not perish, but have eternal life. (John 3:16)

Just a Thought

Prone to wander, prone to stray
Away from where I ought to stay.
What was that? Did I hear You say
That you still love me anyway?
It's hard to believe, but could it be
That I have value in just being me?

The Twinkle in God's Eye

The twinkle in God's eye reflects
the love He has for man.
A love so big and beautiful
it's hard to understand.

The twinkle in God's eye reflects
the heart of His desire,
that all would come and none would perish
in the lake of fire.

The twinkle in God's eye reflects
the truth of His spoken Word,
And through His word the promise
of everlasting life is heard.

The twinkle in God's eye reflects
the joy He wants to give,
to us, a joy that overflows
when we ask Him to forgive.

The twinkle in God's eye reflects
the pain He did endure,
when He sent His Son to die for all
who'd ask to be made pure.

The twinkle in God's eye reflects
the tears He has for some,
for though they hear Him calling,
to His arms they will not come.

"The Twinkle in God's Eye" scripture references

> *For I am convinced that neither death nor life, neither angels nor demons, neither the present nor the future, nor any powers, neither height nor depth, nor anything else in all creation, will be able to separate us from the love of God that is in Christ Jesus our Lord. (Romans 8:38–39)*

> *For God so loved the world that he gave his one and only son, that whoever believes in him shall not perish but have eternal life. (John 3:16)*

> *And the devil, who deceived them, was thrown into the lake of burning sulfur, where the beast and the false prophet had been thrown. They will be tormented day and night forever and ever. (Revelation 20:10)*

> *Then death and Hades were thrown into the lake of fire. The lake of fire is the second death. If anyone's name was not found written in the book of life, he was thrown into the lake of fire. (Revelation 20:14–15)*

> *In the beginning was the Word, and the word was with God, and the Word was God. He was with God in the beginning. (John 1:1–2)*

> *The Word became flesh and made his dwelling among us. We have seen his glory, the glory of the One and Only, who came from the Father, full of grace and truth. (John 1:14)*

> *I am the way and the truth and the life. No one comes to the Father except through me. (John 14:6)*

I have told you this so that my joy may be in you and that your joy may be complete. (John 15:11)

This righteousness from God comes through faith in Jesus Christ to all who believe. There is no difference, for all have sinned and fall short of the glory of God, and are justified freely by his grace through the redemption that came by Christ Jesus. God presented him as a sacrifice of atonement, through faith in his blood. (Romans 3:22–25)

On hearing this Jesus said to them, "It is not the healthy who need a doctor, but the sick. I have not come to call the righteous, but sinners." (Mark 2:17)

All day long I have held out my hands to a disobedient and obstinate people. (Romans 10:21)

Only a Heartbeat Away

May I be with You, Lord.
To feel Your heart
To lean on Your breast and sigh.

May I rest in Your shadow
Feel Your wings touching me
Keep me only a heartbeat away.

Your face I behold
But it's Your heart that I seek.
That I know and feel Your desire.

To feel Your breath on my face
As I breathe in,
Keep me only a heartbeat away.

May my prayers offer up
A pleasing scent to You, Lord.
May Your Holy Spirit be pleased.

May I understand
The lessons You teach.
Keep me only a heartbeat away.

May the rhythm of Your heart
Inspire me to love
More deeply than I've ever loved before.

Let the sound of Your heart
teach me to sing
Of Your great love forever more.

Lord, hear me, draw me,
reach out for me please.
I want to be held in Your loving embrace.

May I drink in Your scent,
May my whole life be spent.
Only a heartbeat away.

Worship Me Not

Animals saw that people had carved from stone
Their images and they were put on display.
But to their shock they watched as the people
Bowed down to the images to pray.

"Worship us not," cried the beasts to the people,
"For we are created beings.
Direct your worship to the Creator God.
To Jesus Christ our King!"

The Earth saw the people gathering her goods
To use whenever they'd please.
But to her horror she watched as the people
Gave thanks to her down on their knees.

"Worship me not," cried the Earth to the people,
"For I am a created thing.
Direct your worship to the Creator God.
To Jesus Christ our King!"

The stars saw the people giving honor to them
As if they gave wisdom along with their light.
And the stars started crying, for all of them knew
That though wrong, people thought they were right.

"Worship us not," cried the stars to the people,
"For we are created things.
Direct your worship to the Creator God.
To Jesus Christ our King!"

SECTION 2

Miracles and the Lessons I Learned from Everyday Life

Driving Lesson

When I was a little girl, I dreamed of traveling around the country following the roads that intrigued me, and I wanted to go down each one. Where did they go? What glorious wonder would I find at the end?

As a child, I was overweight, shy, and introverted. I was teased and made fun of often. Others had the power to humiliate. Others had authority over me.

At eighteen years of age, I learned to drive an eighteen-wheeler, and I began traveling across forty-eight states of the United States fulfilling my dream. Oh, the power. I never realized how grand it felt. And authority? It appeared that I commanded it wherever I went in the cab of that truck. I was seated above everyone else, and I imagined that my peers admired me. On the road, others had to yield to me because I was bigger, stronger, and more powerful than they, and I took advantage of it whenever I could. Now it seemed that I had the power. I had the authority.

When I was twenty, out on a Northern California highway, in a convoy with other trucks, I was at the peak of feeling that power. The tractor at my command had a 400 Detroit motor. My trailer was empty and light. Those rolling California hills caused the other truckers to slow down as they climbed to the top of them and then try to regain some speed on the down side to make climbing the next hill easier. I passed several trucks, rejoicing that for once, I didn't have to slow down and then speed up again with them.

But my joy that day didn't last long. After passing another truck, I moved into the right lane again. As I did so, two boys in a Hot Rod Camaro passed me. They couldn't have been any older than me at the time. They continued on ahead and passed the truck in front of me and then pulled in front of him. We were at the top of yet another hill, and the boys in the Camaro slowed way down and would not let that truck gain speed. Nor did they move out of the way. By the time we got to the bottom of the hill, this truck had to climb the hill in lower gears. This not only slowed the truck but slowed the traffic behind him and could disrupt the schedule all truckers need to keep. I listened to the frustration of the truckers on the CB radio as I passed both the truck and the boys in the Camaro again. The boys continued to play their game and again passed me and then pulled in front of me, slowing down. I moved out to pass them, but they quickly moved out into the left lane preventing me from passing, and therefore, I too had to downshift to keep from hitting them. They raced on ahead and proceeded to play their game with yet another truck.

Needless to say, I became very angry. My adrenaline started flowing, and my reasoning fled as I pulled that truck out into the left lane and pushed that powerful eighteen-wheeler to ninety miles per hour to catch them. It didn't take long. They were slowing yet one more truck. They must have seen me coming because they pulled into the fast lane as I approached. But we were clear of the truck they slowed, and the traffic on the interstate was light, so I darted back into the right lane, not missing a beat. I passed them in a blinding speed, blasting the air horn all the way. As they sped up to prevent me from passing them on the right, I purposely started to move back into the passing lane when the tires of my trailer were right next to their car, effectively moving them into the grassy median that divided the highway. Needless to say, I was pleased with myself. When they caught up to me again, I arrogantly straddled the line preventing them from passing. Every time they tried to come up next to me and pass, my trailer was over that line, keeping them from getting in front of me. They finally gave up and got off at the next exit, probably hating trucks now more than ever.

Even as I write this, forty years later, I am appalled at myself. Both of our actions were potentially deadly. But mine were worse. I had the greater power. Being bigger, I commanded more authority. But being the *professional driver*, I had the greatest responsibility. Being given so much power at a very young age, I thought I knew what was best, and no one had better mess with me. I was arrogant and self-righteous about driving.

It was not long after this that the Holy Spirit started speaking to me about that incident and the attitude of my heart as well as the responsibility I carried as a driver. He brought scripture to mind such as Proverbs 14:29, "Whoever is patient has great understanding, but one who is quick-tempered displays foolishness." And also Matthew 20:25–28,

> But Jesus called them to Himself and said, "You know that the rulers of the Gentiles lord it over them, and *their* great men exercise authority over them. It is not this way among you, but whoever wishes to become great among you shall be your servant, and whoever wishes to be first among you shall be your slave; just as the Son of Man did not come to be served, but to serve, and to give His life a ransom for many."

And during my years of driving, as I grew older and learned about that responsibility, I became gentle and meek when on the road. Through experience of seeing wreckage and death on the road, I learned to let others have the advantage and didn't push my way in. For the great power and weight behind me could crush an ordinary vehicle and those inside it. I made room for others and gave them the benefit of the doubt. I didn't become angry or insist on having my way. I strove to become finely skilled at handling that vehicle in every situation.

Over the years, I began to realize that driving trucks and the anointing and gifts of the Holy Spirit are similar. Gifts are powerful and, when anointed, have authority. But you cannot just mow people over with them or push them the way you want to go because you have them. You can hurt people, quite unintentionally, from youthful zeal and unskilled handling of these anointed gifts from God. It seems to me that most people are a lot like automobiles on the highway of life. They only know their little part of the road. In some ways, the power of God's anointing on a gift is like these big trucks. Most people don't give trucks or truckers any thought, except when one slows them down that is in their way. That truck could be carrying the very thing that person in the car will need that day or the next—food, clothing, or medicine—but all the person sees is something getting in the way of where they want to go.

God is like that. He anoints people with His authority and His power. and many times, those very people are misunderstood. They have been given gifts from God to impart to others, but they seem to get in the way of the very people God wants to bless. Heavy anointings are often misunderstood and ridiculed. They are also misused by those not used to the power and authority granted.

As you are gifted with anointing for the work the Lord has prepared for you, be patient and humble. Take the time to become skilled at operating in that gift.

A Prayer for a Truck

Lord, would you bless that great big truck,
that runs on diesel and a little bit of luck?

And bless all the tires that grip the ground,
that take it across country and then back to town.

Please bless the engine that runs so "sweet,"
underneath that iron heap.

But, Lord, most of all, would you please bless
the driver of that great big mess.

The Miracle of Teleportation

I woke up in Spokane, Washington, in the sleeper berth of my eighteen-wheeler parked at the fueling station of the Flying J truck stop. It was 10:00 p.m. and my usual time to rise and shine, hop behind the wheel, and drive for the next eight hours. But I was not looking forward to it this time. Even though I had tried to sleep for the past several hours, I had tossed and turned and was unable to rest. I was still very tired.

My husband finished fueling the truck, and I finished dressing. We parked in the lot and went inside to pay and have something to eat—dinner for him, breakfast for me. I remember Spokane at that time for the baked potato I had ordered. It was as big as a dinner plate covered in chili and cheese, and in just one word, *delicious*. Oh, and coffee—I drank lots of it.

I thought that eating my food and drinking my coffee would wake me up and get me to feeling chipper, and it did, for about twenty minutes. The heavy meal and the already feeling of sleepiness were difficult to fight off.

We walked back out to the truck in that cool summer air of 1984, and I got the bidder stick out and went around the truck to bang on each tire to make sure they were sound and all in good shape. I checked the hose connections of air and lights to make sure they were secure. I know we had just done this, but I thought routine would help me wake up more.

I climbed in the cab and marked my logbook up to date and turned on the motor, looked at the map to see where I was to go as my husband climbed into the sleeper berth of the truck and said good night. All things seemed in order, so I steered our truck out of the Flying J parking lot and onto Interstate 90 east. As I entered the interstate, I saw a sign that read "Missoula 188 miles." In my mind, that was about four hours, and I needed to drive to at least Butte before I could pawn the driving off to my husband again. Butte, Montana, was about two hours past Missoula.

It was not long before I saw another sign saying "Welcome to Idaho" and, after that, "Coeur d'Alene 12 miles." Okay, that sounded fine. I would stop there and get another cup of coffee, walk around the truck, and I would be okay for a bit. But Coeur d'Alene came and went with no off-ramp that I could see where I could easily bring my rig off and then back on. So I continued on past the town and started the long drive up the mountain passes.

The first pass was called Fourth of July. The weight of the fully loaded truck caused it to slow, and I downshifted. As the truck slowly climbed the hill, I got sleepier, so I blinked and reached out for the CB radio. I turned it on. I heard only a few people talking now and then, so I turned on the regular radio, but the music made me want to sleep, and the talk shows were worse! I rolled down the window, but that did not help because even in the summer, the mountain air got too cold. Almost to the top of the grade, I felt my head nod, and I jerked it back up, widening my eyes and rolling the window down again. I heard light talk on the CB about road construction ahead of me, and about that time, I saw the signs to be prepared for two-way traffic. I also saw a sign for a truck stop in Kellogg, the next town ahead, and I looked forward to that cup or two of coffee. But I must have nodded for a second time for I looked again, and I was past the exit. I watched it slowly disappear in my side-view mirror, and I was frustrated that I had missed it.

But I kept going, and in a few minutes, I started to hear a voice that sounded like a group of people saying the same thing together.

"Jennifer, you need to pull over. You are falling asleep."

And I argued back, "I know, but there is no overpass that I can park under. I have to keep going."

And keep going I did. I remember another sign, "Wallace next exit" and, at the same time, "Road Construction Ahead" with arrows directing the traffic to cross over to the left lanes and enter into two-way oncoming traffic. I remember blurry headlights coming toward me and people on the CB radio talking about looking out for someone crossing into oncoming lanes and that they are all over the road. I didn't know it then but know now that they must have been talking about me.

Again the voices said to me, "Jennifer, you need to pull over. You are falling asleep."

And I argued right back, "I know, but there is no overpass that I can park under."

I kept trying to drive. I passed another road sign saying I passed the town of Mullan, and my motor started to slow and strain, so I knew I had to downshift. I was beginning the climb of Lookout Pass.

The voices again said to me, almost yelling this time, "Jennifer, you need to pull over. You are falling asleep."

And I argued back again, "I know, but there is no overpass that I can park under."

What seemed to be a minute later, I was looking at a sign passing over my head on an overpass that said I had reached Lookout Pass, the top of the mountain and the dividing line between Idaho and Montana, and I was despairing that I had not seen it sooner, so I could not stop under it and rest.

The voices said to me for the final time, "Jennifer, you are asleep."

I woke up at dawn, facing east with the sun about to come over the top of the mountain. I was parked perfectly at the side of the road under an overpass just west of the city of Butte, Montana, and just before the I-90 and I-15 interchange. My truck was still idling, the running lights were on, and the parking brake was set. I was still in the driver seat staring at the beautiful sunrise. I had no idea how I got there. I pushed it aside and woke up my husband because we were now in Butte, and I could go to sleep.

About fifteen years later, I moved to Coeur d'Alene, Idaho. I had forgotten this incident as a young driver until I had occasion to visit my mother for the first time after moving to that beautiful state. She lived in Bozeman, Montana, and I was excited to see the countryside. As I started up Fourth of July Pass, I remembered nothing about that night. I saw the little truck stop in Kellogg and actually stopped there for a cool drink and a snack. I continued on to the historic little town of Wallace, and the interstate now was no longer under construction, but it was mostly all elevated with bridges and high walls that seemed to go over the town. When I was there that sleepy night, they had been constructing the elevated bridge section of the eastbound lane. All traffic had been diverted to the westbound side of the road which was also elevated above the town.

I continued on to Mullan, Idaho, and I remember that sign so well. I don't remember why because there was nothing out of the ordinary about that sign, just a memory. It seemed I had seen this sign before. The road became steep, and even in my little Geo, I knew I was climbing up to Lookout Pass. What I did not remember and that I now saw was that the road was divided in the middle by concrete barriers and was full of curves. On the right were high mountain sides and on the left, steep dizzying cliffs. Then I reached the top, and I saw the sign declaring that I reached the mountain time zone as well as Lookout Pass and still I did not really remember. I did notice there was no place for a car, let alone a big rig, to just stop and park for a while.

Next was the "Welcome to Montana" on a small billboard and cautions for trucks to be careful. Winding roads with S curves and 45-mph limits were posted with flashing yellow lights. Signs with a truck tipping over if not careful and 6 percent grades were everywhere.

I saw a rest-area sign and decided to take a small break for I had been driving about two hours. The air up there is some of the most wonderful air you can inhale into your lungs, and the beauty of the mountains has stayed in my heart. I wanted to stay for a while and explore, but it was only a rest area, and I wanted to get to Mom's house before dark, so onward I went.

After about thirty miles, a truck weigh station waited for all trucks to enter and be weighed for safety, checked for logbook and license compliance.

I drove my little Geo in wonder at the beauty of this state as every mile passed, and I remembered none of it. Even if I had remembered that I had been there, it would have been dark. I had been there at night. Four hours later, after driving on long stretches of highway and even more winding canyons, I approached Butte, Montana. I drove under an overpass and recognized the mountains in front of me, and as if God had opened my memory, I suddenly remembered them as the same ones I woke to over fifteen years ago.

I was more than a little shaken as the memory of that whole sleepy night came rushing back to me, and I needed to pull over at the nearest place and get a cup of coffee and to think.

As I sat in the little café, I remembered the whole story up to and until Lookout Pass and then nothing. I remembered the voices, that I now believe to be my guardian angels, telling me that I was falling asleep, and that later, I was asleep. My heart was racing, and it was not the coffee. I realized that a miracle had taken place fifteen years ago, and I did not even know it.

I remembered waking up at the side of the road as safe as could be with the sun rising in the east. I had fallen asleep at the wheel of an eighteen-wheeler, and I was saved from the real possibility of a deadly crash. But how did I get from Lookout Pass, Idaho, to Butte, Montana, that night? Who drove? Who parked the truck and turned off the headlights, leaving only the running lights on? How did I get past all those dangerous curves, and who downshifted and, using trailer brakes, kept the truck under control on the 6 percent grades? How did I get past the ever-open and always-present weigh station?

I had not been pursuing God at that time, though I prayed from time to time and read my Bible when I could. Being in my twenties, I thought mainly about me, what I liked and what I wanted. But God saved my life and allowed me to be transported to the very town I needed to be in for the end of my shift and in record time.

Record time. Please allow me to explain this further mystery for it is wonderful what the Lord, who is outside space and time, has done.

From Spokane, Washington, to Butte, Montana, is about 316 miles according to online maps and distance calculators. For a car traveling at legal speeds and not stopping for anything, it will take you about six hours. An eighteen-wheeler will take longer for they must climb mountain passes in lower gears and then use those lower gears to get back down on steep grades. They must go slower around curves to stay upright and stop at any and all weigh stations that are open. You can add up to another hour for them. So we are looking at seven hours of nonstop travel for me to get from Spokane to Butte.

Add to that, I woke that night a 10:00 p.m. and was at the truck stop for about an hour, fueling and having dinner in the restaurant before leaving Spokane. So about 11:00 p.m., I started on my trip.

In the mid-summer months in the northern parts of Washington, Idaho, and Montana, the sun can rise as early as four thirty in the morning. So from the time I started driving until the time I woke when the sun was coming up was a total of five and a half hours. But how long had I been parked there, asleep under that overpass before I woke to that glorious sunrise? Minutes? Hours? I do not know. Even now it is a mystery to me except to say that I know that God must have transported me and saved me for a purpose.

I think of Philip in the Bible and how God translated him after he talked to and then baptized the eunuch in the desert. "And when they came out of the water, the Spirit of the Lord snatched Philip away; and the eunuch no longer saw him but went on his way rejoicing. But Philip found himself at Azotus and as he passed through he kept preaching the gospel to all the cities until he came to Caesarea" (Acts 8:39–40).

I had done nothing at that time in my life that would have moved God to translate me. I was not preaching or teaching or even spending much time with Him. How can I sum this up? What can I say but that I know God does wonderful, miraculous things for ordinary people for reasons known only to Him and that He will reveal the answers when and if He chooses to do so. Even as I write this, I know there are no ordinary people, for every single one of us on this planet are special to God.

And like the Apostle Paul says in Romans 8:35, "Who will separate us from the love of Christ? Will tribulation, or distress, or persecution, or famine, or nakedness, or peril, or sword?" And in Romans 8:38–39, "For I am convinced that neither death, nor life, nor angels, nor principalities, nor things present, nor things to come, nor powers, nor height, nor depth, nor any other created thing, will be able to separate us from the love of God, which is in Christ Jesus our Lord."

So many things have happened in the thirty-seven years of my life since this time. Some wonderful, some terrifying and painful, and through each one, I remember this time and the wonder and love of God. And every time I do, my faith flares up, refreshed and strong, for I know my Redeemer lives. Perhaps that was the reason all along—to remember how great and awesome the God of creation is, to share with others about His grace and that I am loved. And so are you!

LESSON FROM A BABY GOAT

It was in the summer of 2001 at the county fair that I witnessed for the first time an animal-judging contest. It was a hot Saturday afternoon, and my sister and I set up our chairs in a shady location. We settled down to eat our shaved ice snow cones, while children and their show goats were walking around getting ready for the judging.

The first class entered the ring. I watched as the children and goats walked in a circle around the judge, making sure to have the animal between themselves and the judge. My heart went out to one young girl as she tried to show her baby pigmy goat. The baby was tired and hot and did not want to cooperate. Every few steps, the little goat would bleat in protest and fall over on its side. The girl ever so gently righted the little animal and again tried to walk forward.

Time after time as every few steps the animal would fall, she would gently lift him to his feet and start again. She never lost her temper or became impatient. She spoke quietly to him as she kept her eyes on the judge. When the judge finally made his decision, this young lady and her baby goat came in fourth out of six. The judge explained that he was impressed at how gently she had handled her animal and never lost her temper but was always encouraging it.

The following morning at church during worship, the Lord reminded me of this young lady and her little goat, and I was overcome by emotion. Most of the time, I feel like this baby goat—tired of struggles, uncooperative, not understanding what is required of me, and wanting to go home. But the Lord, like the little girl, is patient and full of encouragement and understanding.

He is always ready to pick me up and set me on my feet, always encouraging me to take just one more step because someday soon, the trials on this earth will be over, and I'll be with Him forever.

Thank You, Lord Jesus, that You are full of compassion and grace. I thank You for Your encouragement to me and that You are full of mercy. I love You. Amen.

At the Hen House

I walked with my sister to her hen house on the hill the other day. One of her hens had hatched a single chick a couple of weeks ago, and this was the first time I saw this one. Sister had brought a special treat for her hens, a bag of stale bread. I watched as the chickens scrambled for the bread and pushed each other out of the way so they could get the best pieces for themselves. But the mamma hen would eat a bite and then picked off small pieces of the bread and tossed them to her baby, clucking reassuringly the whole time.

The baby stayed close to mom, and my sister reminded me of how the Lord longs to gather us together as a hen gathers her chicks. But she said she never realized that a hen broke off manageable pieces of food for her babies until this day.

I noticed that my sister wisely fed the mamma and baby separately from the rest of the group. As the other chickens continued to jostle each other for the bread, I thought of how the baby could be hurt or starved if it was in the group. With the other grown chickens and no protection from the mother, this baby would probably die.

Isn't this how it is with us? When we give our hearts to Jesus, He encourages us to stay under the Father's wings of protection. As we stay in His word, He feeds us manageable-sized pieces of the Bread of Life. If we stray from His protection, we can be trampled by others, incurring wounds that can hurt us or even kill our faith. Stay close to Jesus, like this baby chick, until the day we are mature. Allow His Spirit to nourish you as you read His word and, even then, continue to abide in the shelter of His wings.

The Smallest of Things

I have always liked lizards. It appears to me that they always have a smug smile on their face as if to say they are content in whatever circumstance they find themselves. Or they know something funny about living that I don't. Anyway, they have always fascinated me.

One day, the neighbor's cat caught one of these little creatures. This particular lizard was of the variety that could lose a tail in an attempt to confuse the enemy and escape to freedom, later regrowing its tail. But on this day, the ploy did not work on this wily cat, and the feline had every intention of making this lizard its lunch. Sitting on the front porch, resting from its pursuit of the lizard, the cat looked up at me as if to say, "See what I am having for lunch? Do I not deserve praise for my hard work? Pet me please!"

Needless to say, I dropped what I was holding and rescued the lizard from a most horrible death. Where its tail had been was a mess, and it had a few cuts from the claws and teeth of the hungry feline. But its main trouble was exhaustion. So I created a terrarium for the little beast and nursed it back to health.

After a few months of caring for this mini dinosaur, the tail started to grow back, and he (I will call it a he because I don't know how to tell girl lizards from boy lizards) was once again healthy. My husband and I became greatly attached to him as a pet, and making sure he had fresh water, meal worms, and crickets from the pet shop was a priority. But after those few months, we began to imagine that the little smile on the lizard's face was not so smiley. I began to think that it was lonely and needed to be back in the wild again, with its own kind. I told my husband that I thought we should let him go.

We worried about other cats capturing him again if we were to let him go in the yard. We worried that he would not find food or water if we took him to another part of the countryside. For several days, we agonized over the place we should let this little charge of ours go.

Finally, my husband and I decided on the brush in the canyon a few miles up the road from our home. Many times we had walked to this area but had never seen a lizard. We carefully placed the small creature in a plastic travel container for such animals, got in the car, and drove to the place of decision. We prayed out loud for the Lord to care for this little animal, and my heart was aching.

As we drove into the large dirt lot, the morning sun was just coming over the hilltops, and most of the area was still in shadow. But one spot, about the size of a basketball, was ablaze with the sunlight. And in the center of this sunspot was a wild lizard of the exact species of the one we were returning to the wild, only this one had its original undamaged tail. I was thrilled but expected it to run away up into the brush the moment I stepped out of the car and moved toward it.

But it stayed right there in the sunlight, unconcerned. I slowly lowered the travel container to the ground about a foot away from the wild lizard, amazed that it still had not run away, and let my little charge walk out when it was ready. It didn't take long for him to test the air and meet the wild lizard that turned slowly after the meeting and casually sauntered out of the sunspot and up the hill into the brush, our little friend happily following.

It was as if the wild lizard had been instructed to wait and meet our charge and escort him back to the wilderness. It only took a few moments, but my husband and I stared at each other, knowing in our hearts that the Lord Jesus heard our prayer and knew the concern and compassion we had for this seemingly insignificant creature. I had tears in my eyes as I realized that Jesus truly does care about the things we care about, even the smallest of things.

Once again, I praise you, Jesus!

SECTION 3

Short Story Parables of the Love of God.

A Lesson Learned

"He is cruel. Power and thunder come forth from his scepter. All free creatures are to be warned and be afraid of him. Death almost always comes to those who cross his path, and yet I have heard of his mercy. You never know which will kill and which will choose to bestow mercy, so don't be tricked. Be safe, my young one, and stay away from him. Stay away from them all!"

That was my father's warning about the princes of the earth from the day I was born. But I had never seen one of whom he spoke. How can one believe in something they have not seen? Stories I supposed to keep us from misbehaving or just plain old-fashioned folklore. I didn't know and wasn't sure I believed him. What did the old ones know anyway? But then again…maybe being young, we should not carelessly discard the wisdom of what our parents try to teach us. Anyway…

Late one evening, as the sun was setting, and the sky was brilliant with color, I prepared to eat my supper. I was hungry and tired for I had a long day filled with trying to dig out my first new burrow. I stretched sore muscles and had just settled down to eat when out of nowhere, I heard the growl. It was sinister. It was evil. And it was *close*!

The hair on my body raised on end as a shiver of fear and the feeling of doom ran through me. Because I was tired, I had let down my guard, and I knew now I was in trouble. My heart started pounding, my breath I held one moment and gasped out the next! Where was it? From which direction did it come? My eyes darted here and there, my ears swiveling to catch the direction of the sound, and then, *there*! To my left, the face I recognized as evil. The face of death. An archenemy. A *weasel*!

In an instant, I turned to my right and started running as fast as my four legs would carry me. "Dodge to the left," I screamed to myself, "then back to the right. Remember your training! I can't! Just run. Leap over that bush. Don't stop! Don't stop!"

I could hear him gaining ground, laughing and growling, his breath blowing on my heels! This was a game to him. He enjoyed causing my panic, and I was helpless to stop him! Oh, help me, someone! Help *me*!

Suddenly, the weasel was there in front of me. He lunged, and his razor-sharp teeth slicing away just missed my face. I screamed in terror, and flipping in midair, I dashed away the way I had come. Partially blinded by fear and sweat, my legs shaking and aching and weak, my chest burning, I know I can't run anymore. I...I...can't.

What is *that*? On the path ahead of me, I know in my heart stands another deadly creature. A giant, standing there on two legs with a scepter in his arms, perfectly still. "Oh, Father, your stories were true. I see a man." Deeper fear and dread fell upon me. My mind was racing, but I realized now there was nowhere left to turn. *I'm dead anyway*, I thought. "But I don't want to die by a weasel. I will run to the feet of the man and die by his hand, *not* the weasel. He will be defeated, robbed of me, his prize!" So be it.

I ran with what little strength I had left, gasping for every last breath, until I collapsed between the feet of this prince of the earth. I closed my eyes for my time had come. I waited, resigned to my fate.

My enemy stopped. I heard him gasp in surprise and frustration. I felt the man move. Here it is, the end. Suddenly, thunder and lightning burst forth from the scepter carried by the man, and though frozen by terror and exhaustion, my eyes flew open, and I saw an explosion of fire and dirt hit my enemy. The weasel flew away in mortal pain, and I was left there in the sudden silence, hearing only my heartbeat and breathing as they began to slow down.

I then heard a low, soft sound, unlike anything I had heard before. Where was it coming from, the man? He just stood there while I rested on his feet. He continued his sounds, and they seemed to bring me peace. I felt comforted and then stronger. I gathered my courage and started to move. I wasn't sure if this prince was friend or foe, but I sat up and then looked up at the man. He looked back at me and continued his sounds. I stood and then slowly walked away. The man didn't move, and after a few feet, the sounds stopped, and I turned to look back at this man once again. He was, as my father said, very tall, with a scepter of power in his hand. But this day, for me, this prince of the earth withheld the scepter of death from me and extended mercy. He turned and walked away from me without another sound. I too turned and disappeared back into the forest.

Since that time, I have reconsidered my father's teaching because of my experience. I believe those things I was taught and have begun teaching them, along with my own testimony to others as well. I am still very afraid of the princes of the earth, but to the one who was merciful and saved me, I thank you from the bottom of my heart for reflecting the true King of the earth and bringing hope to us free creatures that someday, along with the earth, we will all be redeemed and restored and that we will live in peace with each other under the reign of the True King, and there will be no more crying, no more fear, and no more death.

A. Bunny

Remembering

I fell in love, I thought with a dream.
His coat was pure white, glittering clean.

His eyes were so beautiful, loving yet wise.
I thought he was wonderful, giant in size.

His heart must have been as big as the world.
The hair on his face was a little bit curled.

The power he mustered at just a mere whim
Made me stand staring in awe at him.

I stand in this meadow and look at that hill
And remember the way that he first made me feel.

To think that he loved me is an answer to prayer
For he was a unicorn, I, just a mare.

THE SAW BLADE

In the dark corner of an old storage shed, hidden from view, lay an old rusty handsaw. The handle was broken and had been wrapped with baling wire in an attempt to keep it together. Its blade was dull and had a few broken teeth. Rust was forming along the surface, and it had long ago been considered unusable. So thrown into this dark little corner, covered with dirt and oil, the old rusty handsaw, full of despair, was resigned to the fact that it would never again be used for the purpose it was originally created.

For years it lay in the corner of that shed, never seeing the light of day and only dreaming what it had been. But one day, the door opened, and the master came in and started looking for something. The little saw heard him rummaging around in the old shed. He sighed, knowing it could not be for him. But light started to break through into the corner where he lay, and he heard the master cry, "I thought it was lost, but it has been found!" The master excitedly picked up the little handsaw and brushed off the dirt. "Oh," he said, "this is perfect."

The little handsaw was incredulous, so full of doubt. *I am not perfect*, he thought. *The master has made a mistake. My teeth are dull. I can no longer cut anything. My handle is broken. I am worthless.*

But the master lifted him from the darkness and took the little saw into his house. Little by little, the master began his work as he started cleaning off the rust and the dirt. Then he buffed and polished until all the rust was gone. He was coated with a protecting sealant, and then as hours turned to days, brush strokes from a paintbrush in the hand of the master tickled the little saw. He was amazed at how much time the master spent with him. The little blade could do nothing but yield to the master. The handle was left as it was, broken and held together with wire. The teeth were still chipped and dull, and he carried the evidence of the scars of hard work and abuses in his life. But before long, under the hand of the master, there was a beautiful painting with bright colors intricately painted on his side.

Through the reflection of the master's eye he saw that he had become more than what he was in the beginning of his life.

The little handsaw thought he was of no value because he was old and broken, could no longer be used for his original purpose, and left abandoned in the dark corner of a shed for what seemed years. But the master had a plan for the little saw from the beginning. He kept the little saw until the time was right, and with the work of his creative hand, transformed the broken saw into a beautiful work of art and was now lovingly hung in the master's house, and with new purpose, he would be admired and enjoyed by all forever.

Ivy the Dragon

CHAPTER 1

Deep in the swampland, right in the middle, lived a very large family of dragons. With a grandfather and grandmother, fathers and mothers, brothers and sisters, aunts, uncles, and so many cousins, they couldn't always keep track. Yet everyone knew the youngest was Ivy.

None of the other swampland creatures trusted the dragons. They were known for taking things that did not belong to them, and they had a nasty habit of having their neighbors for lunch. Nobody slept much either for the roaring and hissing, arguing and fighting. And the dreadful dragon songs were endless. It seemed there was never a moment of peace in the swamp where the dragons lived.

On rare occasions, Grandfather Dragon would tell the story about a shepherd who lived in a valley high in the distant mountains. He told how the sheep that lived there had been placed under a horrible wicked spell by the shepherd, and how he had made slaves of them all. He claimed that the sheep were too stupid to know any better, and they fell for his tricks. Now they had to stay with him forever and do whatever he commanded them to do.

This story always excited the younger dragons because they loved to bully and pick on others who were weaker than they were. They wanted to go up the mountains and see for themselves how stupid the sheep were and to laugh and make fun of them. Ivy wanted to go too, but her brothers and sisters said they didn't want a baby hanging around spoiling all their fun. Her cousins felt the same way and told her to go home. Ivy complained to her mother and father, but they told her to stop whining and went about their business. So Ivy made up her mind that she would secretly follow her brothers and sisters up to the mountain valley. It took them most of the day. Everything in their path either ran for cover or flew away to escape the dragons' careless passing. The dragons stomped on the bushes, knocked over small trees, and muddied every stream of water they came to. The other creatures were angry at the dragons and complained bitterly, but the dragons just laughed at them. They didn't care who they hurt or what they broke.

As Ivy followed at a distance, she began listening to the other creatures for the first time. She had always been right in the center of the family group whenever they traveled about and had never seen or heard anyone else. Her brothers and sisters always told her how dimwitted all the other animals were for not getting out of their way. Ivy had always laughed right along with them. Now that she was by herself, things appeared different. She watched the other creatures grieving over their homes that had been stepped on. She saw the nests with the little baby birds that had fallen to the ground, and it tugged at her heart. She told herself that she was a dragon, and that these things were not supposed to matter. But the closer she got to the valley in the mountains, the more miserable and confused she became.

It wasn't hard for Ivy to follow the trail of destruction left behind by her family. By the time she reached the mountain valley, she wasn't at all sure if she should have come in the first place. Doubts about who she was and an unfamiliar feeling of compassion for her fellow creatures was just about more than she could handle. She was almost positive that she didn't want to see any mysterious shepherd or any sheep stupid enough to fall under his spell. Just as she turned to go back down the mountain, she heard laughter fill with contempt. Ivy had caught up to her brothers, Bark and Timber. They were crouched on an overhang, looking out on a beautiful valley where a flock of sheep grazed quietly.

"See how those sheep keep looking over to the shepherd? They must have to get permission first before they can do anything," said Bark with a bit of sarcasm. He curled his lips back away from his teeth as if smelling something bad. "What a bunch of feather brains they are for getting caught!"

Timber shuddered and hissed, "Oh, how can they stand so much quiet! I'd go out of my mind if I had to be that quiet!"

As the two brothers continued to laugh and make jokes about the sheep, they looked out over the valley. Ivy crept in carefully so she could see too.

"Hey, look over there!" said Timber.

On the other side of the hill, near the edge of the valley, Ivy's sisters and cousins, about two dozens in all, were snapping their jaws together as loud as they could in hopes of scaring the sheep. The sheep nearest to the dragons stopped their eating and talking to watch the show. But their lack of fear irritated the dragons so much. They started hissing, spitting, and whispering to the sheep that they looked mighty tasty and how hungry they all were after their travels from the swamp. They sheep turned around without a word and headed straight for the shepherd. The dragons laughed at them, thinking that they were running away in fright. But the sheep heard the shepherd's voice calling to them, and without a moment of hesitation, obeyed.

Bark and Timber rolled with laughter at the obedience of the sheep. They too thought the sheep had been frightened and started making more rude jokes about them.

Ivy hadn't seen any fear in the sheep and said so to Bark. Her brother spun around in surprise at her voice, and being furious at the fact that she followed him up the mountain, he bit her on the shoulder.

"That's because you are too stupid to know anything!" he growled at her.

Timber accused her of not paying close enough attention, and then both brothers started to laugh at her as large tears formed in her eyes. She backed away from the overhang to escape her brother's vicious ridicule.

I too was paying attention, she thought to herself. *And they were not afraid.*

Ivy decided to find a place where she could watch the sheep by herself for a while. Her family kept up their noisy conversations and rude laughter. Some of her sisters crept around to the other side of the flock and let out bloodcurdling screams. The sheep opened their mouths to call for the shepherd, but before one word passed their lips, the shepherd appeared, seemingly out of nowhere, and gave Ivy's sisters a bump on their heads with his staff. He then skillfully moved his flock away from where the dragons had been hiding. The sisters were outraged at being caught and started blaming one another. Ivy giggled to herself.

She continued to watch the sheep walking to and from the shepherd. To her, it appeared they liked him. He reached down and gently touched them. He held the little ones in his arms. They played right there with him, and he laughed. Only it wasn't like her family when they laughed. They always laughed at her, not with her. Ivy was drawn ever closer to the flock of sheep.

Why were they so happy? Her grandfather said they were slaves caught in a wicked spell. He claimed that the sheep had to do whatever the shepherd commanded of them. Yet whenever the shepherd asked any of them to do something, they were joyful about it and seemed eager to please him. The difference between Grandfather's story and what she was seeing just didn't seem to make sense. She found a bush close to the sheep and crawled underneath. With her nose and eyes just barely sticking out from under the leaves, she resumed her study of the sheep. Only the more she watched, the more questions she had. The sheep didn't argue or fight among themselves. There was singing, but it was soft and lighthearted and directed to the shepherd. They shared what possessions they had with each other. It was very peaceful here, and it was something Ivy was beginning to like very much. She was even beginning to like the sheep. They didn't look stupid to her.

Several hours passed, and the sun had set behind the mountains. Long shadows crept across the valley, and Ivy's family had given up their harassment of the sheep. It wasn't any fun trying to scare someone who just wouldn't scare. They all decided to go back down the mountain to their home in the swamp, and on their way, everyone agreed that Grandfather was right. The sheep were stupid. Being caught in a wicked spell from "that horrible shepherd," as the sisters put it, was just what they all deserved.

Nobody noticed that Ivy was not with them. Nor did anyone care. Dragons, being very selfish, only cared what happened to them. It was way too much trouble to worry about someone else.

Ivy was still under the bush, watching the shepherd and the flock as they settled down to sleep. She was thinking about her family and how they were always fighting. No one seemed to care about her the way this shepherd cared about these sheep. Just then a small bird flew into her bush to sleep. Finding a dragon was the last thing he expected and froze in terror at finding one there. Ivy turned her head very carefully and whispered gently that he was safe, and she wouldn't hurt him. He was welcome to stay there as long as he pleased. The little bird didn't believe her, and Ivy was sorry she was a dragon. Dragons lied to everyone about everything and thought nothing of it. Lying never bothered her before. Yet tonight, not being trusted broke her heart. The little bird gathered his courage and flew away. Ivy had never before felt so alone. She determined that when morning came, that somehow she would find out more about the shepherd. With that on her mind, she curled up and went to sleep.

A thin bright beam of sunlight shining through the leaves woke Ivy. She couldn't remember having a better night of rest. As she began to stretch and yawn, she froze. Right in front of the bush where she was hiding grazed a very small lamb whose name was Lily. Ivy was very uncomfortable stretched out, with her mouth open and all, but she was afraid that the lamb would see her and give her hiding place away. She didn't want the shepherd to rap her on the head the way he had her sisters the day before. As she carefully closed her mouth, the lamb spotted the movement.

The lamb, thinking that the dragon was there to cause problems, looked directly at Ivy, and without a hint of fear, boldly questioned, "Why are you hiding in that bush?" Ivy was so surprised that she couldn't answer. The lamb then commanded, "Come out of that bush right now and be gone!"

Ivy started to cry. Huge dragon tears rolled down her cheeks. It was the lamb's turn to be surprised. She moved closer to the bush and carefully asked, "Why are you crying, dragon?"

Ivy sniffed a little and said, "Please don't make me leave. My name is Ivy, and I've just got to know why you and the other sheep stay here with the shepherd. Did he cast a wicked spell on you to make you stay here? Why are you all so happy? What kind of songs were you singing, and why were you singing them? Why weren't you afraid of my brothers and sisters or any of my cousins? Why aren't you afraid of me?"

"Why we stay with the shepherd?" echoed the lamb. "Wicked spell…what wicked spell?

Ivy retold the story she heard from her grandfather and the events that happened since yesterday when she left the swamp. She apologized for the way her family acted. The lamb paid close attention to everything Ivy told her, and when she was finished, Lily said, "Well, you have been through quite a lot, but I must beg your pardon. Your grandfather is mistaken. There is no wicked spell. All of us in this valley have chosen freely to live here. When the shepherd called to us, we came. We were not forced to come, and now I call him my shepherd. I never seem to need anything. He takes me to wonderful pastures in different parts of the valley that are cool and green, to beautiful still ponds of clear sweet water. When I am tired, I rest in his arms, and he makes me feel strong again. He guides me in the things I need to know, like what is right and wrong. He encourages me to do the right things for his sake, for he is so good. Even though at times enemies lurk around that would try to kill me or eat me, like your brothers and sisters, I am not afraid because the shepherd is with me all the time. He is always watching and protecting me. And sometimes I do things I know I'm not supposed to do, and he is swift in chastening me with his staff. But that is a great comfort to me, especially because I know he wouldn't discipline me if he didn't love me. I know his goodness and love are following me every day of my life, so I choose to stay with him in his valley forever.

"As for the singing, we love to sing praises to him and songs of love because he loved us first and called us to be here."

Ivy then sighed a huge dragon sigh. "That sounds wonderful," she said. "I've been watching all of you since yesterday, and I would love to live here with you, but…" Tears started falling from Ivy's big sad eyes. "You were called here by the shepherd to come and live with him. I wasn't. I came here with my brothers and sisters to make fun of you. And now, after listening to you and seeing things the way they truly are, I don't want to go back to the swamp."

Ivy covered her head with her paws and started crying as if she would never stop. Lily was overcome with compassion for the dragon and looked up to see if the shepherd was near. He was standing on the other side of the flock, but he was looking directly at Lily. When they made eye contact, he knew what she was asking. He smiled and nodded his head. The shepherd knew Lily had a compassionate heart and a bold spirit. He also knew that Ivy had been in the bush all night. It was the shepherd himself that sent Lily over by that bush to have her breakfast. With the nod of his head, he gave Lily permission to bring comfort and hope to the despairing little dragon.

"Oh, Ivy," said Lily. "Please don't cry. Would you like to meet the shepherd for yourself?"

Ivy was suddenly frightened and told Lily so. In this short time, Ivy had begun to trust the little lamb. But the shepherd? She was so afraid of the thought of meeting him she backed up a few steps.

"Do not be afraid," Ivy assured Lily. "The shepherd will not hurt you. He has told us many times that anyone who chooses to come to him, he will not send away. Our shepherd always tells the truth."

Hope began to stir in Ivy. "He won't send me away?" she whispered.

"No," said Lily with a smile. "Come on, let me lead you to him. He is waiting for us now."

Ivy brushed away her tears and took a deep breath. She reminded herself that this is what she wanted to do and that she should not let the opportunity pass her by. She may never get another chance. She crept ever so carefully from under the bush and dusted herself off the best she could. She was caked with mud from living in the swamp and quite dirty from yesterday's travels. After spending the night under a bush, she felt she should try and get clean before meeting the shepherd, but Lily assured her that it was perfectly all right to come to the shepherd just as she was. He would take it upon himself to make her spotlessly clean. So feeling very self-conscious about her appearance, she started to follow Lily across the meadow. Her head was down, and her tail was tucked. Every now and then she would sneak a peek at the other sheep. One by one they lifted their heads to watch the youngest lamb leading a dragon toward the shepherd. One by one each smiled as the two passed and waited expectantly to see what would happen.

As they approached the shepherd, Ivy began to feel safer and less afraid. She started feeling the longing to be next to him growing stronger. When they were finally standing at the feet of the shepherd, she felt as if she never wanted to leave.

The shepherd asked, "What do you want me to do for you?"

Ivy never heard a question asked so gently before. She dared not look up though, for she still felt so dirty. She mustered her courage and replied in a tiny voice, "I no longer want to live with the other dragons, even though they are my family. I desire to stay here in this valley and be with you. I know you didn't call me like you did Lily and the others, but would you make an exception, just this once? I can't bear the thought of returning to the swamp."

The shepherd was still looking at Ivy and asked, "What makes you think that I haven't called you? Didn't you feel the pain of the other animals when they lost their homes? Didn't you feel compassion for the birds that lost their children when their tree was destroyed? That pain and compassion is my heart for all things. The longing you have to remain here is also my heart calling to you. I long for you to stay here with me too."

Ivy was amazed. She looked up at the shepherd for the first time and saw the beaming smile on his face. "But I am a dragon!" she exclaimed. "You've called me, even though I am a dragon?"

All of the sheep in the flock had knowing smiles on their faces. The shepherd too was chuckling with joy over Ivy. "Yes, Ivy. I have called you even though you are a dragon. And so it was with all my sheep." Ivy looked around at the others, and they were all nodding their heads. "Each was a dragon when I called to them. I have called many, but only a few ever come. I have longed for a flock that I could cherish and love. However, I didn't what to force anyone. Because you have come to me and asked to be part of my flock, so be it. From this day forward, I will call you one of my own."

The shepherd reached down and lifted Ivy in his big strong arms. He turned to his flock and announced, "Welcome your new sister!"

Shouts of joy were everywhere, and the sheep were leaping and jumping and thanking the shepherd for yet another sister. Ivy was overwhelmed with acceptance, peace, and love, the likes of which she never knew before. She looked down at Lily and noticed that she was crying. Ivy immediately wanted to know why.

"I was the last one to become a sheep before you came. I have never witnessed the transformation before. It was so beautiful. Look, Ivy, you're clean!"

Ivy looked around at herself and beheld…she was a lamb!

Chapter 2

Ivy stayed close to the shepherd for the next several months, and her joy, understanding, and love for the shepherd increased daily. She followed him into the green pastures Lily told her about, where she would lie down next to the still waters and rest. As she lay there, she'd think about things the shepherd had been teaching her. And as time passed, she began realizing that not only was the shepherd her teacher, provider, and protector, he was her friend.

Occasionally, dragons from different parts of the world would come to watch, tease, or mock the sheep and the shepherd. A few of these dragons would become curious about the sheep, as she had, and would respond to the shepherd calling to them. Ivy loved to watch the transformations, for each one was different, and these dragons would join the flock as newly created lambs. Ivy thought of how she came to be a sheep and looked carefully at all the dragons that came, in hopes that one of her own family would return and hear the shepherd calling to them.

But as the months went by, she became very sad. Oh, not that she was unhappy living there with the shepherd and the other sheep, but it bothered her to think that her family believed a lie. The shepherd was anything but wicked. She began to wish that someone could go back to the swamp and tell them all the truth about the shepherd. And the more she thought about it, the more unhappy she became. The shepherd did not overlook Ivy's loss of joy. So one day as they were walking together through the wildflowers that always grew there, the shepherd asked Ivy what was bothering her.

"Dear Shepherd," said Ivy. "I keep thinking about my family back in the swamp. You know they still believe Grandfather's story about you. It hurts my heart to think about them going through their lives and never knowing the truth. When I lived in the swamp, never was there any peace. Someone was always hurting or in trouble. And love is a word they don't even know. I didn't know it until I met you. My dear Shepherd, they may all die there in that swamp and never get a chance to know that they could live here forever with you! Isn't there something that you could do?"

The shepherd understood how Ivy felt. He stopped walking when he came to a large shady tree and sat down to rest. Ivy crawled up in his arms and waited for him to answer. They stayed in the shade of the tree for a very long time, and when evening drew near, the shepherd gently woke Ivy. She had fallen asleep, trusting that her friend would help.

When she was fully awake and looking directly into his loving face, the shepherd very softly said to her, "Ivy, I am not at liberty to leave here just now. It is the wish of the owner of this valley that I remain and care for those who are here and those who are coming. I choose to do his will, dear one, because he is my Father.

Ivy felt her heart sink down to her toes. Her bottom lip started to tremble, and her disappointment was threatening to overwhelm her. "But"—continued the shepherd as if he was still thinking about his answer—"I could send you."

Ivy's poor heart jumped immediately from her toes just to stick in her throat. It was pounding so hard, and she was breathing so fast that her mouth became dry. Her tongue tried its best to stick to the roof of her mouth as she answered in surprise. "Me? But who am I, dear Shepherd, that I could go and speak to them? I don't know what to say! I am the youngest of them all, and they would never listen to me!"

"I have given this a great deal of thought, Ivy," said the shepherd, "and I know you can do this. I would never ask you to do more than you are capable of. You have been taught all that is necessary to speak the truth to your family. But so you won't feel so afraid, I'll send a helper with you. You go to the others now. I will let you know when it is time to go."

Ivy was relieved. At least she wouldn't have to go back there alone. She hoped that Lily would be the one he chose to go with her. They had become close friends. Ivy ran to the flock and found Lily and told her all about her conversation with the shepherd and that she would be going back to the swamp to tell her family about him. Lily was very concerned.

"Ivy, promise me you'll be very careful. If you are not, you could be tempted to act like a dragon again and slip into the mud. I've heard of it happening to others who went back with very good intentions and have never returned. Once they are in the swamp, they forget all about the shepherd and this valley, and I know that it breaks the shepherd's heart. Even though they are still his sheep, you would never know it by looking at them."

"If the shepherd knew that was going to happen to them," said Ivy with concern growing in her voice, "why did he send them out?"

"That's just the thing," replied Lily. "The shepherd didn't send them. They thought they knew all that was needed to convince their neighbors about him and didn't ask his permission. They just left. The shepherd was very distressed for the longest time. I think he still is. I see him at the crossroad where the mountain pass and the valley come together, waiting for them to come home. He told me one time that he trains each of us for different things to do that we will enjoy and will be capable of carrying out. He told me that some of the other sheep that have gone off alone had not received enough of his teaching. They also left the valley without the helper."

"The helper…" said Ivy slowly. "The shepherd told me that he would send a helper with me so I wouldn't be afraid. Do you know anything about the helper?"

"Yes," replied Lily. "I do know him, and you are going to love him! He will help you remember everything that the shepherd has taught you so far. It is a great thing to have the helper go with you. The shepherd and he couldn't be any closer. Sometimes it's as if they were the same person, only they look different."

"How come I've never seen him?" questioned Ivy.

Lily shrugged her shoulders as an answer, and both lambs started walking to another part of the valley to find clover with blossoms. It was getting close to dinner, and this had become their favorite meal. As they walked, Lily thought about why Ivy hadn't seen the helper yet.

"Maybe you just haven't learned to recognize him," said Lily. "I know that since we became lambs, the helper has been with us every moment, watching over us to make sure we are safe. But don't worry,

Ivy. The shepherd said he would send him with you, so I know it won't be long before you meet him."

Lily and Ivy finished their supper and joined the other sheep at the feet of the shepherd. This was one of Ivy's favorite times of the day. All the sheep would sing songs about the shepherd and about all the things he has done. They would sing songs of love to the shepherd and he too would join right in and sing back to them of how much he loved them. The youngest lambs would take turns being held in his arms, and some of the rowdier sheep would leap and dance around him. A few of the sheep were very quiet and reserved as they sang. After the singing, some in the flock would take turns telling everyone about the things they had been learning from the shepherd, and everyone enjoyed listening. Then all too soon for Ivy's liking, it was time to sleep.

As she curled up with the others under the watchful eyes of the shepherd, she thought about all the things the shepherd told her that day. She wasn't sure if she should have brought up the subject of her family to the shepherd. Did she really want to go back to the swamp to talk to them? What if she was tempted and began to act like a dragon again?

So many questions and fears swirled around in her mind. But the one thing she did not forget was that she loved and trusted the shepherd. He knew what he was doing, and with that truth in her heart, she fell asleep.

Ivy woke early the next morning, and while all the others were still sleeping, she went looking for the shepherd. She never had to look very far for he was always close by, forever watching over them. He was pleased to see Ivy coming to him and welcomed her into his arms. She was still thinking about what Lily told her, and it made her uneasy. The shepherd knew what was bothering her but waited until she spoke.

"Dear Shepherd," Ivy questioned, "will I be all right when I return to the swamp? I'm afraid that I will not be able to do anything right and mess everything up. I'm not sure if I really want to go."

The shepherd smiled at Ivy. "Yes, Ivy, you will be all right if you pay close attention to the helper and depend on the things he tells you. He will not misguide you." The shepherd stroked her forehead. "There may be some things that are difficult to overcome, but you will come back home safely. I can promise you that." The shepherd set Ivy on the grass next to him. "Come with me," he said.

Ivy followed the shepherd to a part of the valley she had never been to. It was beautiful in the early light of dawn. "There is someone I want you to meet today," said the shepherd. "He is the helper who is going to go with you. But I want you to get to know him before you leave."

The shepherd stopped next to the spring which fed the sparkling river that ran through the valley. He looked up, closed his eyes, and spoke in a language that Ivy had never heard before. It was so sweet and pleasant to listen to that Ivy wanted to cry. And then in the blink of an eye, a brilliant white dove flew to the shoulder of the shepherd.

"Ivy," said the shepherd with great joy, "I want you to meet the helper. His name is Promise because I promised you that you would not have to go from the valley alone. Promise will always be with you from now on, and he will help you, teach you, comfort you when you need it, correct you if necessary, and show you what I would have you do. Listen to him just as you would me."

Ivy just stood there looking up in awe at Promise. His feathers glistened like silver. His eyes penetrated her soul, just like the shepherd's did. She was surprisingly comfortable in his presence. As she stood staring at him. He smiled, cleared his throat and said, "Hello, Ivy. You have grown quite a bit since your rebirth as a lamb. It has been my pleasure to watch your progress."

Ivy was stunned. "Have we met, sir?" she questioned in amazement. She was sure they hadn't, but something seemed mighty familiar about him.

"Not formally, my dear, but I've been watching you since you were hatched in the swampland. I've even spoken to you a few times when you were in places that were very dangerous, even for a dragon. And I'm pleased to say, though you didn't know it at the time, you heard me and escaped death more than once."

Ivy just stood there for a few moments. Then she remembered her manners and thanked Promise for his help, though for the life of her, she couldn't think of when those times may have been.

Then she asked, "You were in the swamp when I was little? Why haven't I ever seen you before?"

Promise flew down to a branch on a bush, eye level to Ivy.

"You couldn't see me until you became a lamb, but I followed you everywhere, encouraging you to listen to the shepherd's call. He has loved you since the day you were born."

The shepherd smiled and then excused himself from them and returned to be with the other sheep when they awoke.

Ivy and Promise spent the day together, and Promise recalled several things to Ivy's mind that she had forgotten about or had set aside as not being explainable. And by evening, Ivy was beginning to trust and love Promise as much as she did the shepherd. She was having such a good time getting to know more about him she forgot to eat anything. But Promise reminded her that it was time to eat and accompanied her to her favorite place. She was always amazed that no matter how many times she ate there, by herself or with friends, there were always enough blossoms on the clover. Ivy lost all track of time as hours passed into days and days into weeks.

One afternoon, the shepherd called to Ivy. "It is time for you to begin your journey," he told her. "Promise has informed me that he feels you are ready, and I agree with him. Promise will remind you of everything I taught you and, most of all, that I love you. Listen to Promise. Go wherever he leads you, and nothing will harm you. Do not worry about what you will say to anyone, for Promise will give you the words you need to know at the very time you need them. Do not cause him to become sad, for when he is distressed, so am I."

The shepherd walked with them to where the mouth of the mountain pass met with the edge of the valley floor. "I will watch for you here until you return home."

Just then, Lily came running across the meadow, calling out for Ivy to wait. She had asked the shepherd if she could go with Ivy, but he told her that it was not in his plans for her but not to worry about Ivy. She would be safe as long as she listened to Promise. When the shepherd saw how disappointed Lily was, he invited her to come with him, and together they would watch Ivy leave the valley.

"I am going to miss you Ivy," cried Lily as the two hugged one another tight. "Please be careful and come home soon, okay?"

"I will miss you too, Lily," said Ivy. "I wish you were coming with me. But I'll be all right. I have the shepherd's Promise."

After another long and loving hug, Ivy and Promise set out on the road that would lead them back down to the swamp.

Chapter 3

Promise led Ivy away from the valley, down a road she'd never been on. Next to the road ran a tiny stream of water. It flowed from a spring that had its origin in the center of the shepherd's valley. It was still very early in the morning, and the sunshine that just peaked over the mountaintop was warm on Ivy's back. They stopped after an hour or so to eat breakfast and rest. Ivy stepped over to the little stream to drink and was surprised when a small but familiar-looking bird also flew down to drink. She waited for him to freeze in fear, as every other bird had ever done when they realized they were next to her, but he courteously bid her a good morning. Ivy recognized him at once.

"Good morning," she replied. Since the day she became a lamb, Ivy had not seen any other creature, except Promise, the shepherd, all the other sheep who lived with her, and the dragons that came by from time to time. She was overjoyed that her first encounter was with the very same bird that had been so afraid of her the last night she was a dragon.

"Excuse me please," she said to the bird. "But do you remember me?"

The bird took a long look at Ivy and replied, "You do look familiar, but forgive an old bird, I don't." The bird felt rather embarrassed for not remembering her, but Ivy put him at ease.

"I am, or rather, was the dragon under the bush you flew into one evening several months back up in the valley of the shepherd. I'm afraid that I unintentionally gave you quite a scare."

The little old bird looked even closer at Ivy.

"Well, bless my soul, it is you! And look at you now. You are a beautiful lamb. Congratulations, my dear. You know," he said with a hint of confession, "you did scare the daylights out of me that night. But I learned a valuable lesson. Always pay attention to where you are going, and never take anything for granted. Danger can be anywhere, anytime, and we need to be ready for it, or we could be seriously hurt or killed. You know," he said thoughtfully, "I was sure that I heard the shepherd tell me to rest in that bush for a while. Since that night, I have wondered if I did hear him correctly. You were the last person I expected to find there."

Ivy thought for a moment about what the bird said. The shepherd told him to rest in the very bush she was under. Ivy replied to the bird, "When you flew away in such fright, I was so hurt and felt so alone that I knew I wanted to know the shepherd. I no longer wanted to be a dragon if it meant being so alone. Had it not been for you, I would just have turned around and followed my family back to the swamp."

Both the bird and the lamb looked at each other and huge grins appeared on their faces and comprehension set in. "The shepherd knew all the time!" they said at the same time. And they laughed and praised his name.

"Well, it has been fun chatting with you, my dear," said the bird, "but my missus will be worrying about me if I don't get back soon. Good luck to you. And have a great day!"

Ivy bid him farewell, and he was gone in a flash. She was thrilled at her chance encounter with him. Or was it by chance? She looked up at Promise, but he just smiled at her.

After resting for a little while longer, Promise said it was time to move on. He spread his glittering wings and flew down the road ahead of Ivy, to make sure that the coast was clear. He knew that small pathways in the mountains, like the one they were on, were dangerous to travel even in the bright sunshine. They took their time, and Ivy enjoyed the beauty that surrounded her. Promise kept a watchful eye out for anything unusual and, at the same time, delighted in Ivy's wonder. Ivy had never really noticed the colors of flowers before or took the time to listen to the sound of wind rustling the leaves as it passed through the trees. But though she meant to keep her eyes on Promise as they traveled, it wasn't long before she was captivated by the activities of the ants marching along the road next to her.

How did they carry all those things so much bigger than they were? Where were they going, and where did they come from? She was so entranced by them all she didn't see the little gray clouds coming over the mountaintops. She wasn't paying attention to where she was walking either and was startled when she heard Promise speak to her.

"Ivy," he cautioned, "this is the way. Walk here!"

Ivy had been so caught up in her thoughts about the ants that she failed to see that they had come to a fork in the road. Promise had turned to the right, but she had continued on to the left, following the ants. Ivy felt so ashamed that so soon after starting her journey, she had taken her eyes from Promise.

"Have you already forgotten what the old bird by the stream said to you this morning?" Promise lovingly chided.

Ivy blushed with embarrassment. She had forgotten about this morning, and she did feel silly being caught watching a bunch of ants.

"Just a little bit farther," said Promise, "and we'll stop for the night."

Ivy faithfully kept her eyes on Promise for the rest of the day. The little clouds that had been floating across the sky had been gathering together, and by nightfall, thunder started echoing through the mountains. Ivy was becoming afraid, for as it grew louder and louder, she could see no place that might offer shelter.

"Promise?" said Ivy. "I am afraid of the thunder, and I don't see any place that looks safe around here! What are we going to do?"

Promise assured her that it would be all right but kept moving forward toward the storm. Ivy was tempted to run and find shelter for herself. It looked as though Promise was leading her right into the thick of the forest, a perfect place for the lightning to strike. Promise turned off the pathway and into the thicket.

"Come through here, Ivy," he urged.

Ivy looked at the thick brush she was to push through. The thought of plunging into it went against every shred of common sense she had. She couldn't possibly be safe inside matted underbrush in this storm, but she remembered that the shepherd told her to trust Promise just as if he himself were there with her. As she hesitated, still not sure, a crash of thunder and a flash of lightning sent Ivy headlong into the thicket. To her utter astonishment, she was standing at the entrance of a little cave. She followed Promise to the back without a word. The cave was warm and dry, and she listened to the thunderstorm as it raged outside. She felt rather silly now for being so afraid. She also felt a little guilty for doubting Promise.

The dove flew down next to her. "See," he said with a smile on his face, "I told you everything would be all right."

Ivy saw that Promise was not at all upset by the sudden storm and supposed that she shouldn't have been worrying about the storm or finding shelter. And though she had only been away from the valley for a single day, she was learning to trust even more in the shepherd's Promise.

The following morning, when they emerged from the tiny cave, the storm had passed, leaving everything clean and fresh. The two made their way back to the path and continued on toward the swamp. The stream of water next to the pathway was swollen from the overnight rain. Ivy was beginning to get excited as the landscape became familiar to her. She couldn't wait to tell her mother and father about the shepherd. She wanted them all to know that they had been mistaken about him and that he was the best thing that ever happened to her. Promise felt her excitement, and as they approached the edge of the swamp, he cautioned her to be careful and not to get too close to the mud pits. He reminded her to keep watching him and that he would lead her on the paths of solid ground. Now that she was no longer a dragon, being trapped in the mud could endanger her life. Ivy's excitement calmed a bit after this revelation from Promise.

"I'll be right above you all the time, Ivy," said Promise. "So keep looking up. I won't ever leave you. Your family is very vocal, and my voice is soft. It may be difficult for you to hear me, so listen carefully."

And with that said, Promise flew to higher branches in the trees.

When Ivy arrived at her family den, she noticed that things had not changed very much. Everyone was still bickering and quarreling about nothing. But when they noticed a lamb standing at the entrance to their den, for a moment, you could have heard a pin drop. No one from this swamp had ever seen a lamb this far away from the mountains.

"Who are you, and what do you want!" growled Bark with contempt. He started moving toward her in an alarmingly aggressive manner. Ivy was caught off guard for a moment. She had forgotten that she no longer appeared as a dragon, and it hadn't occurred to her that her family might not recognize her right away.

"It's me, Ivy'!" she exclaimed. "I've come home."

Bark was stopped in his tracks. His eyes narrowed, and he wrinkled his nose as if he smelled something bad.

"I should have known that you were too stupid to escape the spell of that shepherd," he snarled. "And now you have the nerve to return home and make a fool out of yourself and us!"

"That is enough!" bellowed her father as he walloped Bark with his tail.

"Bark, you told us you hadn't seen Ivy and that you didn't know what may have happened to her. We've believed she was dead all these months. You lied to us, but I'll deal with you later."

Bark shivered in fear of his father and slithered to the back of the den, furious at being humiliated in front of the family. He'd get even with Ivy.

Ivy's father turned to her. He was glad to see her, but he was thinking of how he was going to live down the embarrassment of his youngest daughter being a lamb. He decided to try and ignore her prominent change in appearance but even so, he was uncomfortable in her presence.

"Where have you been all this time?" he said to her, though the answer was obvious. "Your mother has been worried over your disappearance." He again shot an angry glance at Bark.

Ivy began to tell her family all of the things that had happened to her since the night Grandfather told the story about the shepherd. She reminded her parents that she did say she wanted to go with everyone else. She described in detail everything about the shepherd and how her life was different now. She insisted that they had all been wrong about him, that he was not evil, and she was not under any spell. When she started to encourage them to come back with her to the valley, Bark exploded in a rage.

"I told you she was under an evil spell!" he bellowed. "I know we'd all have been better off if you had stayed with your precious shepherd, instead of coming back here and spreading you wicked lies!" He stormed past his father, his anger overriding his fear, and left the den. Once on his way out he stated, "I won't stay in the same place with her. Until she's gone, I'm out of here!"

Ivy's mother started crying. Her sisters and the rest of the family were in an uproar. Ivy had no idea that what she longed to share with her family was going to have this kind of effect. Her father roared for everyone to quiet down, and then he addressed his youngest daughter.

"Ivy, this is all fine and good for you if this is what you choose to do with your life. But none of what you say really has any significance for our lives here. I think that from now on, you should just not talk about this to anyone else. You'll just cause more trouble." With that said, he too left the den to find Bark.

Ivy turned around and walked slowly out to a place that used to give her some peace and quiet when she was still a dragon. She sprawled out on the sand and wept.

"Oh, Promise, I didn't know it was going to be like this!" she cried. "No one believed a word I said to them. They all think I'm crazy. Whatever am I going to do now?"

Promise flew down to the sand next to her and brushed the tears from her face with his wing feathers.

"Did they really respond differently than any other time you tried to talk to them?" he asked softly. "The important thing you want to remember is why you came back to the swamp in the first place. Can you tell me what that reason is?"

Ivy sniffed and knitted her eyebrows together in thought. Then she looked right at Promise through teary eyes and said, "To tell them the truth about the shepherd so they might come and live in the valley with him and not die here in the swamp."

"And what did the shepherd say would happen?" urged Promise.

Ivy took a deep breath and responded, "He said not to be surprised if they hated me because of him, and that the truth about him would seem foolish to them."

"And now that this is beginning to happen just as he said it would, what are you supposed to do?" Promise said encouragingly.

Ivy thought for a minute and then said, "Not to lose heart and continue to tell them the truth about him until everyone has heard it and then to come home."

"That is correct," said Promise. "It does not matter if they treat you badly, or even if they don't want you to stay with them anymore. The important thing is that you cared enough about your family to want to come and tell them about the shepherd. You know, the truth about the shepherd has a way of working its way down into a dragon's heart all by itself once it has been proclaimed."

Ivy looked at Promise with grateful eyes and a huge smile. He truly was a comfort to have as a friend. She felt she could continue now with her task at hand. She brushed herself off and returned to the den. When she walked inside, her mother informed her that the whole family had been planning another gathering because it was that time of year. Now that she had returned, she, of course, should be there. It was something Grandfather looked forward to each year, and everyone was obligated to attend. Ivy immediately thought of this as a wonderful opportunity to tell a few in her family about the shepherd, but Ivy's mother interrupted her thoughts by reminding her of what her father told her. She too felt that it would be better if Ivy kept the details of her unfortunate experience to herself. But she couldn't help thinking that this was going to be one miserably explosive evening.

When they all started arriving at the meeting grounds, Ivy noticed how everyone avoided her like a plague. She noticed Bark and a few of her meaner cousins off to the side, fuming about having a lamb in the midst of the family. Some of Ivy's aunts and uncles would shake their heads in pity and tell her parents how sorry they were. Grandfather took one look and pretended not to notice her anymore. He had believed his whole life the story about the sheep being slaves of a wicked shepherd, and her appearance here sorely shook that belief, not to mention that it seemed to make him out to be a liar. He always told everyone that the sheep could never leave that valley, and he hated being proved wrong. Everyone seemed to be whispering, and Ivy thought this was one of the quietest family gatherings she had ever been to. She went off a little ways to be by herself and to speak to Promise.

"Ivy," he said, "tonight, your grandmother is going to ask you to tell about your experience in the valley. Do not be afraid to get up and speak to them no matter what. I'll be right there with you"

Ivy was surprised at his statement and thought to herself that Promise had to be wrong about this. Grandmother never asked anybody anything because grandfather always did the talking at gatherings. As she went back to the clearing and tried to mingle, three of Ivy's oldest cousins surrounded her and moved her off into the brush. After listening to Bark, they were enraged at her audacity to show her sheep face at the gathering. They informed her that it would be better for the whole swamp if she were put out of her misery. All three started laughing.

Bark was watching from behind a boulder. After being humiliated in front of his family and then being thrashed within an inch of his life for lying about his knowledge of Ivy's whereabouts by his father, he went searching for these three distant cousins. Though he wouldn't kill her himself, he knew these three would jump at the chance to kill a lamb. They had never been given the opportunity to do so before, and he knew they would enjoy it. The gathering had been increasing in volume, and the three were sure no one would hear—or care.

As they made their intentions known to Ivy, she remembered what Promise told her about her grandmother's invitation that night, and Promise, like the shepherd, never lied. She knew that her cousins could not succeed, but things did not look good. Fear threatened to overwhelm her as her would-be killers opened their jaws full of razor-sharp teeth. Just when she was sure they were going to end her life, she called out to Promise. He flew around her in a flash of brilliant light, and her wicked cousins were permanently blinded by his brightness. Ivy walked back to the clearing, unharmed. She joyfully thanked Promise for keeping her safe and praised his timeliness.

Bark, who had been watching the whole thing, was overcome with what he had just witnessed. Though he saw it with his own eyes, he couldn't believe it. Unable to see Promise during the encounter, he thought to himself, *How did she do that?* He decided he would watch his little sister closely to discover the power she had.

When she rejoined the gathering, one by one, the dragons would come over to her and talk about nothing. Everyone avoided mentioning her altered appearance, but each was dying to ask her how it happened and how she got back here in this condition. Most of them had never seen a sheep up close before, and the only thing they had ever known about the shepherd was what their grandfather told them at gatherings like this one.

Someone rang a huge bell, and everyone headed for the food pit. Ivy wasn't sure if there was going to be anything there that a lamb could eat, but she ran along to the pit with everyone else. She was pleased to see Aunt Dandelion's famous swamp salad and ate her fill. As a dragon, she never liked greens, but her taste in food began to change after she became a lamb. Aunt Dandelion was very happy to see the bowl nearly empty this year. Her salad had become famous because nobody liked it, but she always made it for the gatherings anyway. Ivy, for one, was grateful.

After dinner was the traditional time for telling stories and sharing things that had happened over the past year. Ivy thought back and remembered that it was after the last gathering she had followed her brothers and sisters up to the Shepherd's Mountain. Grandfather usually called everyone, but he was still upset about Ivy being a lamb and being at the gathering. His pride ran deep, and his ego was very bruised. He refused to speak while she remained in the swamp. Everyone was now angry and blamed Ivy. So to try and keep order, Grandmother spoke.

"I think that because there is such a stir about our youngest member returning home as a…" Ivy's grandmother hesitated. She was having trouble herself with the fact that Ivy had become a lamb. "As a lamb," she continued, "I think it would be interesting if she were to tell us all how it happened."

A murmur swept through the assembly as Ivy boldly walked up to the front. She climbed up on the little hill that overlooked the pit and looked for Promise. She spotted him in the branches of a tree very close to the hill where she stood. Ivy was awed that what he told her about her grandmother came true, just as he said it would. She next sought out her grandfather, and when she found him, she began to speak.

"First of all, I would like to thank Grandfather for sharing the story of the shepherd at our last gathering. If it were not for him, I wouldn't know how to say this. Grandfather?" Ivy waited for him to look up at her. He was so resentful and full of pride that he didn't look up. She continued anyway.

"I love you, Grandfather. I will always love you no matter what."

Her grandfather felt as if he had been hit over the head with a rock. Never before had he heard those words. Tears started forming in his eyes and, not knowing how to respond, moved to a darker area. He was embarrassed by his tears and touched by his granddaughter's words.

"But," she said, "you are mistaken about the shepherd and the sheep who live in the mountain valley."

This statement caused the whole assembly to start yelling and hissing in outrage at Ivy. She tried to speak above their voices but was unsuccessful, and Grandfather left the gathering area.

Just then, Ivy saw Promise flying peacefully over the gathering. He circled effortlessly for a minute or two, and to her surprise, everyone immediately quieted down and waited for her to continue. She recounted everything that happened to her since the day she left them, and they listened to every word. She told them about the shepherd and her friend Lily. She described her friendship with the shepherd's Promise and stated that each and every one of them could freely meet the shepherd and that he was not evil.

She told them that if they stayed in the swamp, they would all die. But if they came back to the valley and met the shepherd for themselves, they would live forever with him. Finally, she told them that she would never regret her decision to be a lamb. And when she finished, she walked back to her place in the pit.

Everyone started talking at once. No one could explain the feeling that came over them at the beginning of her message. Ivy looked up at Promise and smiled. They all had so many questions to ask her.

Promise was right next to her, giving her just the right answers. Many of the dragons didn't believe a word she said and began to encourage others not to listen. She was under the spell of the shepherd, and this was all a trick to make slaves of them. This caused a huge argument to break out, and pandemonium resulted.

Then without warning, an earthquake began to shake the gathering pit, and the sand shifted from solid footing to quicksand. Arguing turned to shouts of fear as several of the dragons were caught in the mire.

"There is no way out!" they yelled. Several started screaming that they were all going to die. Everyone was trying to crawl over everyone else in order to stay out of the quicksand, which meant certain death.

Ivy looked around for Promise and found him still next to her. He urgently whispered in her ear that he would lead her out of the pit on solid ground. He told her to call to the others and follow him. Ivy was again amazed as her voice carried above the clamor of panicky voices.

"Follow *me*!" she yelled at the top of her voice. "I can lead you out of here on solid ground!" She lifted up her eyes to the shepherd's Promise and stepped only where he told her to step. Many of the dragons followed her. Some of them thought she was out of her mind to go the way she was going and went their own way in panic. To their horror, they were caught in the quicksand. None of the other dragons would help another for fear of being caught in the quicksand themselves. Nor could they help because of all the confusion, and most of the dragons died in the pit that night. The ones who followed Ivy escaped from that pit and collapsed in exhaustion when they reached solid ground.

Ivy whispered to Promise her love and gratitude for her safety and for that of the others. As she lay there catching her breath, her cousin Digger approached her slowly, weeping. He fell down next to her and continued crying for a while. Ivy waited for him to speak. Digger looked over at her and said in a quiet, shaky voice, "I know the shepherd too."

He squeezed his eyes shut, waiting for Ivy to blast him for slipping into the mud. But when he heard nothing, he opened his eyes, thinking she had gone. He was surprised to see her looking at him with eyes full of compassion and understanding, so he continued.

"If I had only been bold like you, my father may not have been lost in the quicksand tonight." He paused for a minute, then said, "Ivy, I listened to every word you spoke tonight, and it is all true. I know it. I miss the shepherd so much, and I want to go home, but I've been so bad. I don't think he will ever take me back." Digger again started weeping, and Ivy snuggled closer to her cousin to bring as much comfort as she could.

Then she said, "I have seen the shepherd standing at the crossroads where the mountain pass and the valley meet, waiting for those who left to come home. I know without a doubt that he misses you and would welcome you home again. Digger, will you come back to the valley with me?"

Digger just lay there thinking for a few minutes. He wanted to go home with Ivy and said yes. A few more dragons came over, still shaking, to thank her for helping them. But when she asked if any wanted to go back to the valley with her, they all found excuses and went back to their dens to see what they could salvage. Everyone left, leaving Ivy and Digger alone. Everyone except Bark. He seemed confused as he just stared at Ivy. The look of his face was not readable to her, but it sent a cold chill up her spine. Then he too left.

Promise gently called to Ivy, "Let's go home now. Your work here is finished, and the shepherd is waiting."

Ivy nudged Digger and said, "It's time to go home. The shepherd's Promise will show us the way."

Digger looked up and saw Promise and was overjoyed. Even though Digger was a lamb, you couldn't tell. All the mud and dirt from acting like a dragon made him look like one too. Promise beckoned for them to follow, and they obeyed.

After traveling for a while, Digger kept hearing something in the bushes behind them. He was afraid, but if it were dangerous, Promise would have warned them. Ivy encouraged him not to worry about it, and they continued on. Another hour or so passed, and the rustling could still be heard. Promise told them to wait there for a while. They listened as the rustling grew closer, and they heard branches and twigs when they snapped. Then all of a sudden, a dragon stumbled out of the bushes. It was Bark! He hadn't noticed when the others stopped. He was angry with himself for being discovered and stood there speechless.

"What do you want, Bark?" asked Ivy. She was afraid that he was going to cause more trouble for herself and Digger. She was about to tell him to go home, but Promise gently told her to be still and listen.

"I was watching you tonight when our cousins tried to take your life because I was the one who talked them into it. And I saw what happened to them. I heard what you said at the gathering, and I was the one who started telling everyone not to believe you. I can't explain the feeling that came over me that caused me to be quiet, but I still thought you were crazy. But during the earthquake, you knew exactly where to walk and where not to. You were not afraid like everyone else and I have decided there must be something to this shepherd business and I want to meet him for myself."

Bark finished and stood there defiantly. He was ready to fight his way to this shepherd if necessary. But to his surprise, he saw Ivy and Digger smile. They couldn't believe it. Bark wanted to meet the shepherd? It was a miracle. Promise was smiling too as they all started walking.

It was early in the morning, when the first light of dawn starts to creep over the eastern sky, when the four of them reached the crossroads. Ivy strained to make out the silhouette of the shepherd in the dim light, and to her delight, he was waiting there just as he promised. She raced over to him, and he swept her up in his arms, full of joy.

"Oh, Shepherd," exclaimed Ivy, "Digger has come home with me."

The shepherd put Ivy on the ground and walked over to Digger. His head was down, and he was shaking. "Forgive me, Good Shepherd, I know I have caused you sorrow—"

But before he could say another word, the shepherd wrapped his loving arms around him and danced for joy. The moment the shepherd touched him, his coat became perfectly white again, and there was no doubt that he was a lamb from the shepherd's flock. The shepherd called out to the others and woke them, thrilled with Digger's return. Everyone rejoiced with the shepherd and welcomed Digger home.

"Dear Shepherd," said Ivy. "There is someone I would like you to meet." Ivy beckoned for her brother to come out from behind a rock. Bark shook his head. Now that he was here, he wasn't sure if this was such a good idea. Ivy smiled a sly smile and said, "You're not afraid, are you?"

That stung his dragon pride, and he retorted "Of course not!" though he remained behind the boulder. Then Bark heard the shepherd's gentle voice urging him to draw near, so he cautiously emerged from behind the rock.

As the shepherd beamed a smile, Ivy joyfully announced, "This is my oldest brother, Bark."

"I am very happy to meet you," said the shepherd. And as Bark looked up into the eyes of the shepherd, he was caught in the spell of his never-ending love.

BENEDICTION

Dear Reader,

If you do not know Jesus Christ, or if you know about Him but have never opened you heart to invite Him in, I encourage you to ask Him into your life right now. He is gentle, kind, loving, compassionate, and will never condemn you or forsake you once you become His. You can trust Him completely because He loves you.

Matthew 11:28–30 says, "Come to me, all you who are weary and burdened, and I will give you rest. Take my yoke upon you and learn from me, for I am gentle and humble in heart, and you will find rest for your souls. For my yoke is easy and my burden light."

John 3:17 says, "For God did not send His Son into the world to condemn the world, but to save the world through Him."

Hebrews 13:5 says, "God has said, never will I leave you, never will I forsake you."

All you need to do now is simply pray this prayer:

> Dear Jesus, I confess that I am a sinner, and I know that there is nothing I can do to save myself. But I believe that You came and died in my place and rose again, conquering death to take away my sins. I ask You right now to forgive me, and I invite You to come into my heart and into my life right now. Come, Lord, and be my Savior. Thank You.
>
> In Jesus's name I pray, Amen.

"Everyone who calls on the name of the Lord will be saved," (Acts 2:21).

If you prayed this prayer, I want to welcome you to the family of God, and I want you to know that you have been rescued from eternal death and have passed into life everlasting! Go tell someone that you have made Jesus Christ your Lord today!

Romans 10:8–11 says,

> The Word is near you; it is in your mouth and in your heart, that is, the word of faith we are proclaiming: That if you confess with your mouth, "Jesus is Lord," and believe in your heart that God raised him from the dead, you will be saved. For it is with your heart that you believe and are justified, and it is with your mouth that you confess and are saved. As the Scripture says in Isaiah 28:16, "Anyone who trusts in him will never be put to shame."

God bless you!

ABOUT THE AUTHOR

Jennifer met the Lord in Sunday school at the age of seven years. In her twenties, she had an encounter with the Lord through a near-death experience and have been drawing closer to Him as the years pass.

She have traveled all around the United States and lived in several states.

She now lives in the Mid-South with a wonderful man and two cats, Thomas Patrick and Ashley June.

It is her hope that you find yourself drawing nearer to God as you read this book and be encouraged to keep walking on with Him.